The Glory of the Shia World

The Tale of a Pilgrimage

By

P. M. Sykes, Khan Bahadur Ahmad din Khan

First published in 1910

Published by Left of Brain Books

Copyright © 2023 Left of Brain Books

ISBN 978-1-397-66783-0

First Edition

All rights reserved. No part of this publication may be reproduced, distributed, or transmitted in any form or by any means, including photocopying, recording, or other electronic or mechanical methods, without the prior written permission of the publisher, except in the case of brief quotations permitted by copyright law. Left of Brain Books is a division of Left Of Brain Onboarding Pty Ltd.

PUBLISHER'S PREFACE

About the Book

"This is a slightly fictionalized account of life in Persia (Iran) in the 19th century, capped off by a perilous pilgrimage to the Shiite holy city of Meshed (Mashhad), in the foothills of the mountains that run up to the Zoroastrian Olympus, Damavand. The book is a rare collaboration between a turn of the 20th century English and Persian author. The narrative method presages the classic Oscar Lewis ethnographies of poor Mexican families. In both cases, a straightforward account would have been dangerous because of the repressive nature of the society being studied. This is, on one level, an orientalist conceit of an Englishman writing the life story of a (semi-fictional) Persian from the point of view of a Persian. However, Sykes manages to pull off this literary feat convincingly, even for readers at this later date. He also uses the opportunity as a perfect Swiftian setup to gently satire European civilization, which adds an entire ironic layer to the read.

This long-out-of-print (and quite rare) book is a delightful read, particularly for connoisseurs of travelogues. The Shiite, Sufi, Islamic, and Persian lore and legends which are described here will be of great interest to folklorists. The photographs and other illustrations will be of use to graphic designers, anthropologists and historians. This is obviously a primary source on the architecture of the Mashhad pilgrimage site. Largely unknown to outsiders, this complex has some very spectacular (and gorgeous) structures. Most of all, this book is an eye-opener for westerners interested in the deep culture and history of Iran. "

(Quote from sacred-texts.com)

CONTENTS

PUBLISHER'S PREFACE
PREFATORY NOTE 1
PROLOGUE 2
    MY PARENTAGE AND BIRTH 5
    A CAMPAIGN IN BALUCHISTAN 15
    A PERSIAN ENTERTAINMENT 25
    AN AWFUL TRAGEDY 36
    MY BETROTHAL AND MARRIAGE 46
    KERMAN, THE HEART OF THE WORLD 57
    THE DEATH OF MIRZA HASAN KHAN, MUSTAUFI 69
    MY FIRST MAMURIAT 80
    THE PERSIAN NEW YEAR 90
    THE PILGRIMAGE IS VOWED 104
    YEZD, THE PRISON OF ALEXANDER 113
    ROBBED IN THE LUT 122
    THE ARRIVAL AT THE SACRED THRESHOLD 134
    THE SACRED SHRINE OF THE IMAM RIZA 145
    THE PILGRIMAGE IS ACCEPTED 157
EPILOGUE 168

PREFATORY NOTE

OWING to the fact that a majority of reviewers consider The Glory of the Shia World to be the work of a Persian, whereas it has been written entirely by myself, it seems best to explain the precise position.

I would state frankly that my ambition has been to write a second Haji Baba, which would serve as a true picture of Persia some ten years ago, before constitutional reform appeared on the horizon, just as Morier in his immortal work depicted it in the reign of Fath Ali Shah.

The events take place in parts of Persia and Baluchistan with which I am familiar, and, throughout, I narrate what I have actually seen or heard; though naturally the names and circumstances have been altered.

Khan Bahadur Ahmad Din Khan assisted me to collect information on birth, death, marriage, and the New Year ceremonies. He also described the Meshed Shrine to me and brought me many of the quotations and aphorisms which are scattered about in the book.

I can guarantee the accuracy of the various customs which are described, and my familiarity with the life has helped me to give the standpoint of the Persian, which is so different from our own.

Finally, I did not intend to deceive the reviewers or the reading public any more than Morier did; and I imagined that as the hero proclaimed himself the grandson of "Haji Baba" no further clue was needed. At the same time, for high authorities to consider that my work must have been written by a Persian constitutes high praise.

P. M. SYKES, Major.
H.M.'s Consul-General.

MESHED, 7th January 1911.

PROLOGUE

FROM AN OLD IVORY DAGGER-HILT

(Persian text)

In the name of Allah, the Compassionate, the Merciful

BOUNDLESS praise and countless expressions of gratitude are due and befitting to that Lord of the Universe, in the understanding of the substance of whose nature the intelligence of the Wise and the deep thoughts of the Philosophers are confounded and stupefied.

If dried grass can reach the bottom of the Sea:
Then human intelligence can comprehend the substance of His nature.

Salutations and praise be a sacrifice to the feet of the Presence of the noblest of the Universe and the Epitome of all that exists: the Sovereign who wears the ring, by which he is ordained to be the last Prophet, [1] and who bears the Seal of Prophecy on his back.

Thou wert created before all the Mighty Sovereigns:
Although Thou hast appeared the last,
O the last of the prophets, I know thy nearness to Allah:
Thou hast come late, because thou hast come from a great distance.

Boundless praise and peace be on his innocent descendants and his crowned Vice-regents, who are the Kings of all the world, and of what it contains: especially on His Cousin, Son-in-law, Vice-regent and incomparable Vizier, the Chief of the Mohamedans, the Leader of the Pious, the Victorious Lion of Allah, Ali, son of Abu Talib, on him be Peace! He whose birth place was the House of Allah [2] and whose resting-place was the shoulders of the Prophet. [3]

---

[1] This refers to Mohamed.
[2] This refers to the fact that Ali was actually born inside the haram at Mecca.
[3] The Prophet wished to destroy the idols at Mecca; and, to reach them, Ali mounted on his shoulders.

The "Lion of Allah" has been born,
Whatever there was behind the curtain has appeared.

And thousands of praises be on the eleven descendants, who are the Signs of the Zodiac in the heaven of the Imamate; and more especially upon Ali Ibn Musa, Al-Rita, who is the eighth Imam [1] and the seventh Kibla or point of adoration. [2]

Nurullah Khan, son of Mohamed Husein Khan, of Isfahan by descent, has written these few lines, describing his life and his pilgrimage to the Glory of the Shia World, the Shrine of the holy Imam Riza, on Him be Peace, for the information of the inhabitants of the Seven Climates.

In short this is composed
That our memory may remain.

From my readers, I beseech their prayers and beg that, if they perceive any error or mistake, they will cover it with the eye of forgiveness and overlook it because,

No human being is free from error.

FROM A COPPER LANTERN

---

[1] According to Shia tenets, the Imams were spiritual and temporal successors of the Prophet by divine right.
[2] Mecca, Medina, Najaf, Kerbela, Samira, and Kazimain are the other six Kibla.

MY PARENTAGE AND BIRTH

From the Desert of Nothingness to the Bazaar of Being:
A naked mortal has arrived in search of a shroud.

IN the year of the separation 1276, [1] a poet and a historian, if not the first poet of modern Iran, in the form of the narrator of the following events, or, in other words, I, Nurullah Khan, emerged from the plain of Nothingness into the atmosphere of Being. But before introducing myself to the Possessors of Wisdom of the inhabited quarter of the world I will, in the first place, narrate from what family I am sprung.

The poet says

Supposing your father was a learned man;
What amount of his learning has descended to you?

Whether this verse applies to me or not I will leave to the decision of the reader who reads this narrative to the end; but my present object is simply to show that my father was somebody, and that I am not of those who have not seen their fathers' tablecloth spread. [2]

My paternal grandfather was Haji Abul Hasan Khan [3] who first discovered London [4] to us Persians. He it was, who was instructed by Fath Ali Shah,

---

[1] The Mohamedan era commences from the day on which the Prophet fled from hostile Mecca to friendly Medina. a.h. 1276 = 1859 a.d.

[2] i.e. of low extraction.

[3] This individual was the original of Morier's ever famous "Haji Baba." Haji is the title of honour given to those who have performed the pilgrimage to Mecca.

[4] Persians invariably speak of England by the name of its capital.

may Allah forgive Him! to appear at the Court of the English monarch, where he lost no opportunity of increasing the fame of Persia. In short, thanks to my glorious ancestor, the English believe that Persia is covered with rose gardens where, as world-renowned Hafiz wrote. Indeed, such honours were paid to my ancestor of auspicious fortune, that I have been informed that he was offered the Order of the Jarretière, [1] but declined it—at least he never appears to have brought the insignia of the Order back with him to Iran.

The bulbul at dawn laments to the East wind:
Of the havoc that the rose and its scent made

Upon the death of my honoured ancestor, may Allah pardon him! my father and his brother found that they had only inherited debts, as the deceased Haji had always been a lover of generosity, and had spent everything he possessed, and had even incurred debts during his famous embassy, in order that the name of Persia should be exalted, which object can only be attained by spending money freely. Truly has it been said, "Give money and beat the drum, mounted on the moustachios of a monarch."

So However, generosity in every form is one of the greatest of virtues, as a tradition from the Prophet, on Him be Peace! runs:

"A generous man will not be thrown into hell, although he be a libertine; and a miser will not enter paradise, although he be a saint."

Nor was it long before the two orphans found that friendship is of greater value than pearls of the Sea of Oman, as Fath Ali Khan, Nuri, who was a distant relation of my grandfather and indebted to him for having solved many political puzzles for his benefit, came to our aid. Indeed, he no sooner heard of the sad event than he took both my father and my uncle into the kind lap of his family and treated them as his own sons. As Maulavi says with truth:

Whatever atoms of one stock exist
In heaven or on the earth,
They attract one another like straw and amber.

---

[1] Under this name the Order of the Garter is well known in Persia, and is held to be the highest in the world.

Fath Ali Khan, Nuri, was, my father always declared, of so noble a character, of such prepossessing appearance and of such manly bearing, that the Shah-in-Shah occasionally condescended to term him Darya-i-Nur [1] or "Sea of Light." By such acts did the Kajar Shahs bind their subjects to them with chains of kindness, which are stronger than steel. As the poet says:

My friend has put a cord round my neck, and takes me wherever he wills.

Upon the death of Fath Ali Khan, may Allah forgive him! his son, Mohamed Ismail Khan, continued to show kindness to the two orphans, and when he was appointed the Vizier of Kiumarz Mirza, [2] the Governor-General of Kerman and Baluchistan, my father and uncle accompanied him to that distant province.

Mohamed Ismail Khan was so capable that he soon became Governor-General himself, and, in time, appointed my father, Mohamed Husein Khan, to the Governorship of Mahun; and here, as I have already related, I came out from the world of ease and pleasure into that of pain and pride.

My mother, may Allah forgive her! was the daughter of a Kajar nobleman whose father, after the capture of Kerman by Aga Mohamed Shah, had been given a property belonging to a rebel Khan and had settled down in the province. She was very fond of me and saved me many a castigation at the hands of my father for boyish freaks. Show every reverence to your mothers, O my readers, for, as the Prophet says, "Paradise is at the feet of the mothers."

Now, as I hope to act as an interpreter of the customs of Iran, I will tell you what rules are observed when a woman is on the road to reach her desire. These rules may appear to the ignorant strange; but he should remember that they all are based on experience. As we say: In the first place, she

---

[1] The Darya-i-Nur is the name of one of the most celebrated diamonds in the Persian regalia. Persian monarchs are addicted to mild puns, in which connection Nasir-u-Din Shah wrote that Ballater was well named, being balatar or higher than Aberdeen.

[2] Mirza after a name signifies a prince; before a name it means a man who can read and write.

shows an extraordinary craving to eat charcoal or Armenian earth.[1] Of course, no exertion is allowed, nor may a graveyard be crossed; indeed, it is against the custom for her to enter the kitchen at night, for it is then haunted by Jinns. If, however, a woman in this condition falls into cold water, the eyes of her child will be big and lustrous. Again, should an eclipse of the moon occur during this period, the woman must not look at it; also if, by any mishap, her hands touch her body while the eclipse is on, a black mark is sure to appear on the body of the child.

MOHAMED ISMAIL KHAN, THE VAKIL-UL-MULK

If the bat cannot see in the daylight,
It is not the fault of the sun.

---

[1] This habit of earth eating is widely spread in Asia.

When seven months are passed, a feast is held on an auspicious day. Three basins, containing flour, butter, and sugar respectively, are prepared; on these the woman places her hands, and their contents are distributed, with nuts, to the poor. On this day too the woman is placed facing Mecca, is anointed with rose-water, and blessings are invoked.

After this auspicious ceremony has been concluded, the child's clothes are commenced and, when the confinement is at hand, clods of earth are procured, the opening chapter of the Koran is breathed on to them, and they are then thrown into a well to ensure an easy delivery. A plant, termed "Miriam's hand,"[1] is also thrown into a basin, together with an iron ring, and the patient drinks this efficacious draught. Frequently, too, a woman is asked to forego a portion of her dowry.

When the happy event has taken place, no glass may be brought into the room from fear that its rays might make the child squint; indeed the very word may not be mentioned. Moreover, no one wearing black clothes is allowed to enter.

One very important secret I have kept to the last, and that is that Persian children are finer and fairer than any others, because pomegranate juice is freely imbibed by their mothers, and its wonderful colour is reproduced in the rich blood of their offspring.

On the seventh night the joints of the child are smeared with antimony, and the "Yasin" chapter of the holy Koran is specially written on a scroll with its ends joined. Every one sits in a circle, and the child is passed three times through this scroll which we term "the circle of Yasin." Thus early is an infant imbued with the tenets of our holy religion. Indeed, our customs, of which I have given examples only, are really wonderful in their completeness; and it is, in part, thanks to them that we Iranis need fear no comparison with any other race of people in the world.

My earliest recollections of Mahun relate to its wonderful shrine, and, in my own mind, I think that perhaps its beauty affected my disposition, and helped me to write verses which are considered by the experts of this fine art to be as sweet as sugar and as pleasant as a nightingale. The shrine, you

---

[1] This plant is commonly known as "The rose of Jericho."

must know, was built in honour of Sayyid [1] Nur-u-Din, Shah Namat Ullah, may Allah enlighten his grave, and it is necessary that I should represent to you who he was. Sayyid Nur-u-Din was a descendant of the holy Imam Bakir, and was born at Aleppo. In his extreme youth he began a series of travels, which would alone have made him famous. Indeed, His Holiness not only visited the Shrine of the Commander of the Faithful at Najaf, and of the Prince of the Martyrs, Husein, at Kerbela, but on foot he performed a pilgrimage to the House of Allah at Mecca.

Some years later he travelled to Samarcand, at that time the capital of Amir Timur, [2] who treated the Saint with great distinction, welcoming him in these words:

May the sockets of my eyes be thy nest! Be gracious and dismount, because the house is Thine.

Finally, the Saint condescended to choose Mahun as a place of rest, and, although he honoured distant India by travelling thither to the Court of Ahmad Shah, Bahmani, who prided himself on being the meanest of his disciples, yet, for him, Mahun became his native place, and there he lived many years benefiting the people with his manifold virtues.

Not that he was alone as, apart from his numerous disciples, from the Seven Climates came envoys bearing the presents of mighty sovereigns who thirsted for his prayers and wise advice. Indeed, from India alone, the value of the gifts received by the Saint was so great, and the circle of his disciples had become so extensive, that the jealousy of Shah Rukh, son of Amir Timur, was excited; and, but for the prayers of the pious lady, Gauhar Shad Aga, sacrilegious hands would have taxed the property of His Holiness; but, thanks be to Allah, this disgrace was averted.

A short story about Shah Rukh may not be out of place here. He had ordered an ancient mosque to be pulled down, and was superintending the operation of demolition, when he heard a Darwesh, who was standing close by, laugh loudly.

---

[1] A Sayyid is a descendant of the Prophet by his daughter Fatima, who was married to Ali.
[2] Sc. Tamerlane.

H. R. Sykes, phot.
THE MAHUN SHRINE

On inquiring the cause of this hilarity, the holy man replied: Such were the descendants of the great Amir Timur; and the intercession of the lady was due to the fear of the bad consequences which must follow such insolence, for she knew very well that:

The father used to demolish
The dwellings of the people of Allah:
And the son has not spared
Even the house of Allah.

The rod of Allah makes no noise;
But that if it once strikes,
There is no remedy against it.

Shah Namat Ullah, may Allah keep his grave fragrant! was indeed a great Sufi Saint; but, as it is possible that even some of the wise men of Farangistan do not know exactly what the Sufi system is, I will give some account of it, although orthodox Shias consider it heretical.

Yet Allah knows how many thousands of them, although holding different convictions, are drawn to it: Now a Sufi believes that not only True Being but all Beauty and all Goodness belong to Allah alone; as they say:

He said that I am like a mirror
Polished by my friend. A Turk
Or a Hindu will see in, it
What he himself is.
Allah was and there was
Naught beside Him.

In short, Allah is Pure Being, and all else only exists in so far as the Being of Allah is infused into it. Indeed the heavens and earth, with all they contain, are a manifestation of Him. All pious Mussulmans pray daily and say that there is no God but Allah; but the Sufi holds that there is nothing but Allah. Higher than this no human brain can soar; and, to illustrate the nobility of a Sufi's thoughts, I will quote a few lines from Jami, who is considered to be a great exponent of the Sufi system. He wrote:

Whatever heart
Doth yield to Love, He charms it. In His love
The heart hath life. Longing for Him, the soul
Hath victory. That heart which seems to love
The fair ones of this world, loves Him alone.
Beware! Say not, "He is All-Beautiful,
And we His lovers!" Thou art but the glass,
And He the Face confronting it which casts
Its image in the mirror. He alone
Is manifest, and thou in truth art hid. [1]

---

[1] I would take this opportunity to acknowledge my deep indebtedness to the works of Professor E. G. Browne.

As to the Saint's prophetic greatness, I will merely mention that, some years ago, it was one of his prophecies which caused a revolt of the Indians against the English in Hindustan. This potent prophecy ran as follows:

Fire-worship for a hundred years,
A century of Christ and tears;
Then the true God shall come again,
And every infidel be slain.

The path of Allah is concealed, and it is not possible to say why He decreed that the English should have prevailed; but one thing I have heard, which is that the Sikhs, who were very warlike, aided the English because of a prophecy of their great Guru, Tig Bahadur.

This spiritual teacher was imprisoned by the Moghul Emperor Aurungzeb, and was condemned to death for daring to gaze at the walls of the women's apartments of that bigot.

When summoned to receive his doom, the Guru—by Allah, although a Kafir, he was a brave man!—said, "O King, I looked not at the walls of thy women's apartments; but beyond, across the great sea to a distant land in the west, whence a white, fair-haired race will come to avenge me."

Perhaps Allah the All-Wise hindered the fulfilment of the prophecy of Shah Namat Ullah, owing to the tyranny of Aurungzeb, which was wholly without justification. Indeed, even to-day, in Iran this stony-hearted sovereign is cursed by all Shias, for not only the Sikhs, but also pious Shias and the Sufis, all suffered from his lack of inward light in matters divine. Ignorant must he have been of the beautiful lines:

Come back, come back, whatever Thou mayest be,
Whether Thou art an infidel, a fire-worshipper, or an idolater.
This Threshold of Ours is not a Threshold of Despair.
If Thou hast broken thy oath even a hundred times, come back.

I will now describe to you the shrine, which is entered by a fine gateway, supported by two minarets. Traversing a court, built by Mohamed, Shah of Persia, a second court leads up to the tomb, which is surrounded by a covered gallery and surmounted by a blue dome.

HAZRAT ALI SLAYS MARHAB. From the collection of Major Sykes

Shah Abbas constructed the western gallery; but the Saint is buried beneath the dome, and Shah Ahmad Bahmani honoured himself by constructing this building. The doors are of exquisitely carved sandal-wood, and open on to a lovely court with cypresses and flowers planted round a vast double tank of limpid water.

Here, every evening, the learned Custodian of the shrine loved to receive visitors from every Mussulman land, and here, from my earliest boyhood, I came to drink in the pearls of discourse, and to gaze on the beauty of the tiles, the greenery, and the running water. At that time, Allah knows, I understood not why the spot was so dear to me; but, in later days, when I travelled, I always felt that there was some perfection in Mahun which cannot be equalled elsewhere in Iran.

A DESIGN FROM OLD POTTERY

A CAMPAIGN IN BALUCHISTAN

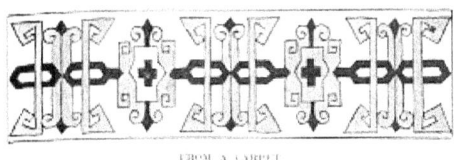

"The Baluch are a people with savage faces, evil hearts, and neither morals nor manners."— Mukaddasi

I had just reached my fourteenth year when my father was summoned to Kerman, where he remained for several days. Upon his return he informed us that he had been appointed as Commissioner to settle the affairs of Baluchistan, which were in a most disordered condition.

Now perhaps you do not know that, owing to its deserts, its savage people, and its remoteness, Baluchistan had only recently been subdued by the victorious Shah, Nasir-u-Din. In consequence, the Baluchis, hating Persians both as their conquerors and the introducers of civilisation, had rebelled and were besieging the Persian Governor in the fort of Bampur.

Fortunately Bampur was strong, well provided with supplies, and occupied by a considerable garrison; but, as the wild Baluchis had assembled in their thousands, and had beaten back army after army sent to relieve the fort, the garrison began to lose heart, praying "for a hand to appear from the Unseen."

The Governor-General wisely decided to send a strong force, with many guns, which the Baluchis especially fear; and, even more wisely, he appointed my father to command it. For, during the years that he was Governor at Mahun, my father, who was of immense stature, by his activity, his faultless marksmanship in hitting an egg while at full gallop, and, above all, by his courage, had made such a reputation for himself that men compared him to Rustam, and swore that he too would have rescued

Bijen out of a well, or performed any other of those great feats that have made Rustam's name famous throughout the Seven Climates.

A Khan once asked my father how it was that he who was the son of a man of letters always displayed such extraordinary bravery and all other qualities of the men of the sword. He replied, "One day, when I was sixteen years old, I was reading poetry, and by chance I read these lines: He added, "I was so fired by these verses, which I kept repeating hourly to myself, that ever since I have been proof against all fear."

If lordship lies within the lion's jaws,
Go, risk it, and from those dread portals seize
Such straight-confronting death as men desire,
Or riches, greatness, rank, and lasting ease.

By Allah! few men had such a father as I have had! As the poet says:

If you want to succeed to the inheritance of your father,
Acquire your father's attainments.

A week was spent in making arrangements for transport, in arming and clothing the whole party, and also in packing up large supplies, not only of cartridges, but also of tea, sugar, and other stores, for, in Baluchistan, not even a packet of candles can be purchased. During all this time I had been begging my father's chief servants to intercede for me to be allowed to go in his service, and, at last, to my joy, my father, who rarely spoke to me, said, "Dost thou wish to see the deserts of Baluchistan?" I replied, "Whatever Your Excellency orders I obey."

My father thought for a while and then said, "How can I expose a raw youth like thou art to the hardships of such a journey? " Whereupon I made bold to quote the following verse:

If thou art not a lion, do not pass through a lion-infested jungle,
For many a brave man is sweltering in his own blood there.

Much travelling is needed to season rawness.

I could have quoted more fine verses but was overcome with shame. My father, however, seemed pleased and remarked, "Thou, my son, art indeed raw; but Inshallah, the sun, the desert, and the hardships will season thee." Thus my father ordered, and, although my mother wept continuously for three days, it was all in vain; indeed it only made my father angry.

We quitted Mahun before the winter set in, and, consequently, we felt it quite hot when we reached Bam, where I saw date-palms and orange trees for the first time in my life. Our party was met by the general of the troops and one hundred sowars; and two infantry regiments lined the river-bed which divides the town into two quarters.

For some days we halted to make final arrangements for the large force, of which my father had now assumed the supreme command, and, as I was without work, I spent the time in studying the history of Bam and visiting its famous buildings, for thus early did my love of history show itself.

Chief among the sights of Bam is the famous fort, which is considered to be the strongest and the loftiest in the world, and, indeed, after carefully examining it, I think that this is proved. In short, as the verse runs:

A fort so high that if the sky should try to have a look at its towers, the golden crown will fall from its head.

I accompanied my father when he inspected it, and, even before the outer gate was entered, a steep ascent cut in the rock had to be traversed. The outside wall, which rose above us to a great height, was passed by means of a gate fit for Rustam's house; but, to my surprise, we only entered a narrow lane, and saw a second wall even higher than the first, rising up almost out of sight.

After proceeding for some distance we saw vast stables, and then entered the main part of the fort by an equally formidable gate up a still steeper incline. Passing the rows of great cannon, we had yet a still harder climb through a subterranean passage to the summit of the fort, where the sleepless commander kept watch and ward.

Here we were shown a well, dug by the king of the Divs at the order of the great Rustam, who vanquished them. Close by was a set of rooms, opening in every direction, and known as a Chahar Fasl or "Four Seasons," where breakfast was served.

I rejoiced at seeing this, as I had been frightened and my head had turned round from awe of this stronghold; but soon I felt happy and proud that the Shah, may Allah make his reign eternal! possessed such a fort, which the savage Baluchis see from their lairs in their naked deserts, and tremble at the majesty and might of Nasir-u-Din Shah, the Sun of Kings, the Ornament of the Country, and the Pride of the Crown and Throne.

My father, who had twice before travelled in Baluchistan, pointed out the peak of Kuh-i-Bazman, distant some forty farsakhs; [1] but so high is it, and withal of so elegant a shape, that there is no mountain in Persia to equal it in beauty. They say that, on its summit, is a shrine to Khedr or Khizr, [2] he who guides the steps of the wayfarer; but few among mortals have ascended there. Indeed, as only Baluchis, who climb like goats, could scale the peak, which resembles a sugar loaf, I cannot vouch for the accuracy of this statement; but, at any rate, by them the peerless mountain is termed Kuh-i-Khedr-i-Zinda, or "The hill of the Living Khedr."

Perhaps, O my readers, you are not acquainted with the story of how Khizr was deputed by Allah the Omnipotent to instruct the prophet Musa or Moses. For he, being lifted up with pride at his own knowledge and wisdom, asked of Allah whether there was any one in the worldwiser than himself. Allah reprehended him for his vanity, and acquainted him with the fact that Khizr was wiser than he was; and bade him to go to a place where the two seas meet.

There he found Khizr and said unto him, "Shall I follow thee, that thou mayest teach me part of that which thou hast been taught?" But Khizr replied, "Verily thou canst not bear with me: for how canst thou patiently suffer those things, the meaning whereof thou dost not comprehend?"

However, Musa begged him and Khizr agreed, on the condition that no questions should be asked until he himself explained his reasons.

So they both went to the sea shore and entered into a ship, in which Khizr made a hole. To this Musa objected, saying, "Hast thou made a hole therein to drown those on board?" Khizr rebuked Musa, who excused himself for breaking the agreement.

---

[1] A farsakh is about four miles.
[2] Khedr is the Arabic, and Khizr the Persian form.

They then left the ship and proceeded by land until they met a youth, whom Khizr immediately slew. This again aroused Musa to remonstrate, and Khizr answered that they must separate, but that first he would explain his acts.

The vessel, he said, belonged to certain poor men who gained their living by the sea; and he had made it unserviceable because there was a king behind them, whose emissaries were seizing every sound ship. As to the youth, his parents were true believers, whereas he was an unbeliever; and so he was killed to save his parents suffering from his perverseness and ingratitude.

Finally, he said, "I did not what thou hast seen of mine own will, but by the direction of Allah."

We left Bam early one morning and the whole town accompanied us for a farsakh on the road, many of the women weeping as if their husbands were already dead, so evil a reputation does Baluchistan bear. As the Arab poet wrote:

O Allah, seeing Thou hast created Baluchistan,
What need was there of conceiving Hell?

For two stages, however, we travelled through delightful jungles full of game, and how I enjoyed being allowed to ride near my father, and to shoot at the francolin as they rose out of the thickets. Indeed I thought that if Baluchistan was at all like Narmashir, it was a delightful country.

However, on the fourth day after leaving Bam, the jungle suddenly ended, and we looked across such a sterile, naked desert that my gallbladder felt as if it had burst. Indeed, even at the first stage the supply of water was the greatest difficulty, as my father had arranged for 700 camels to carry forage and provisions; but to cross fifty farsakhs of desert where there is only a small well at each stage is very difficult.

In fact, that night there was a quarrel between the Narmashir sowars and my father's servants, which nearly became serious; but His Excellency heard of it and, when he came up, every one stopped fighting. As they say:

When the lion appears, the jackal is silent.

For ten days we crossed the dry, empty desert, and although we never saw a human being, there was no fear of our losing the way, as every mile we rode we passed the dead body of a camel or of a donkey. Occasionally, too, we saw the corpses of men whose strength had failed them between the wells.

However, everything at last comes to an end, and, when we sighted in the distance the thick jungle which grows on the banks of the Bampur river, we forgot all about the Baluchis and thought that we had reached the garden of Shaddad. [1]

My father, like the man of experience he was, gave orders that a strong party of sowars should go ahead at early dawn in three parallel bodies, as he feared an ambush; and this was very fortunate, as one of the parties of sowars under Colonel Mohamed Ali Khan, seeing no signs of the enemy, went down to the river and watered their horses without taking any precautions.

The Baluchis, however, were in ambush, and fired on them, killing and wounding twenty men, and had not the other two parties come to the rescue there would have been a disaster. My father was so angry with the colonel that that night he ate [2] five hundred sticks and was ill for weeks afterwards.

We halted for some days at Kuchgardan to rest the troops, whom my father encouraged daily to distinguish themselves by addressing them, and by having passages read from the Shah Nama, in which the exploits of all the heroes of Iran are recounted; and, by Allah! were all Persian generals like His Excellency, no army would ever stand before the victorious troops of the Shah.

While we were halting at this stage, Nawab Khan, Bamari, and his tribe, who alone of Baluchis are Shias, and who are thus loyal to the Shah, joined our camp, and informed His Excellency that Sirdar [3] Husein Khan, Nahrui,

---

[1] A legendary garden lost to human gaze.
[2] To "eat sticks" is to receive the bastinado.
[3] Sirdar is a title signifying a high chief in Baluchistan.

who was the leader of the Baluchis, was camped Baluchis, quite careless at night. He thus advised that he should be surprised in the dark. My father, however, like Iskandar Zulkarnain,[1] replied that he would not steal a victory; and indeed he sent Sirdar Husein Khan a stern message, to the effect that either he and his men must come immediately with their hands bound and throw themselves at his feet, or else, within three days, their bodies would become food for the crows and kites. Within a few hours came back the reply that the Sirdar was awaiting the honour of receiving a guest!

SIRDAR HUSEIN KHAN AND HIS FAMILY

---

[1] Sc. Alexander the Great. Zulkarnain signifies "Lord of two horns," an epithet implying might.

A farsakh from Bampur fort, and was, like all Baluchis, quite careless at night. He thus advised that he should be surprised in the dark. My father, however, like Iskandar Zulkarnain,[1] replied that he would not steal a victory; and indeed he sent Sirdar Husein Khan a stern message, to the effect that either he and his men must come immediately with their hands bound and throw themselves at his feet, or else, within three days, their bodies would become food for the crows and kites. Within a few hours came back the reply that the Sirdar was awaiting the honour of receiving a guest!

My father, who knew that the Baluchis would try to ambush his army, as they had done successfully before in the case of two Persian forces, decided to ambush the ambuscaders.

He therefore arranged that the infantry and artillery with the baggage should march along the main road through the jungle under Suliman Khan, while he himself with the sowars left the camp at night, and, after marching towards Bam for a short distance, took a wide detour and formed an ambush close to where the main body would pass.

In the morning his spies reported that the whole force of the Baluchis was in ambush, exactly as he had anticipated; and very soon shooting was heard and cries of alarm from the main body, which was being attacked.

My father then mounted Raksh,[2] his great war-horse, and, turning round, his face was so terrible with his eyes blood-red, that I felt that to be killed by Baluchis was nothing to arousing my father's wrath. In short, that face inspired us all to become devotees of death, and, charging through the jungle, we fell on the Baluchis, who felt sure that this, the third Persian army, was already their prey.

I followed behind my father, and saw him with one stroke cut the son of the Sirdar into two pieces, just as Amir,[3] on him be peace! cleft Marhab of Khaybar with his famous sword, Zulfikar.

---

[1] A farsakh is about four miles.
[2] The name of Rustam's famous charger.
[3] Amir is the title by which Ali is referred to by Shias, signifying thereby that he is the commander of the Faithful.

This sight threw the enemy into a panic and they all rushed to their riding camels, for Baluchis always fight on foot. Nawab Khan, however, had already seized the camels, and so their only hope was to scatter and hide like rats; and this they did, being chased by the victorious Persians, who did not slacken the pursuit until their horses fell from fatigue and their sword-hilts stuck to their hands.

My father offered ten thousand tomans for the head of the rebellious Sirdar; but he escaped towards Rudbar, and it was not until a month later that it was reported that he had died of his wounds in the desert. Thus may Allahdestroy all rebels against the ever-victorious Shah!

In the evening we rode on to Bampur, but it was not until we drew quite close that the gates were opened and a handful of fever-stricken shadows tottered out to welcome us. One of these was Haji Sohrab Khan, the lion-hearted defender, whom my father at first did not recognise. When he knew who he was he threw himself off his horse and embraced him, and all of us wept to hear that only fifty men of the garrison of six hundred were alive, and that, had the dogs of Baluchis assaulted the fort, instead of merely blockading it, a calamity would have occurred.

THE FORT OF THE REBEL BALUCH

My father ordered the camp to be pitched outside the fort; and I remember with dread how, without even washing his hands, which were reeking with blood, he ordered food to be served without delay.

In a month the justice of my father had drawn the Baluch Sirdars to his footstool, and they represented that they had been led astray and now repented deeply. His Excellency replied, "Allah forgives the repentant sinners"; and as he saw that their hearts were as water, and that they would not rebel again, he showedcondescension to them and forgave them their wickedness.

At the same time he took hostages from every tribe, and thus, with increased dignity, enhanced reputation, and great honour, he returned to Kerman, where the Vakil-ul-Mulk treated him as his son, and the Shah honoured him with the high title of Shuja-u-Saltana or "The Champion of the State"; and Allah knows that this title was befitting, and its bestowal proved that the Shah was ever on the look-out to reward valour and zeal displayed in the royal service.

HEAD FROM A BIRJAND CARPET

A PERSIAN ENTERTAINMENT

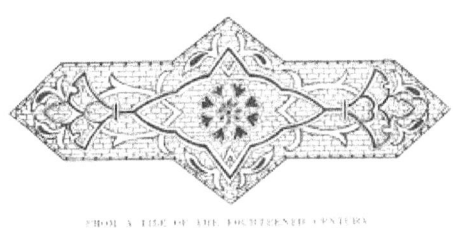

FROM A TILE OF THE FOURTEENTH CENTURY

> Bring wine! let first the hand of Hafiz
> The cheery cup embrace!
> Yet only upon one condition
> No word beyond this place!
> HAFIZ.

ABOUT a month after our return from the war in Baluchistan, His Excellency the Vakil-ul-Mulk informed my father that he would honour him by being his guest at luncheon on the following Friday.

This information threw the entire household into a state of great excitement; and when it is remembered that the Vakil-ul-Mulk never honoured a Khan with an escort of less than three hundred sowars, apart from the nobles of the province who were in attendance, and who also had their retinues, it may be understood that even to provide accommodation for so many people and forage for so many horses was, in itself, a heavy task; and that heavy task was laid on me.

However, thanks be to Allah, the garden at Mahun was fitted to receive even such a distinguished guest as the Vakil-ul-Mulk; and, since it is one of the famous gardens of Persia, itself a land most famous for gardens, it is right that I should describe its beauties to you.

LAILA AND MAJNUN.
From the collection of Major Sykes.

We Persians, whenever possible, build our gardens on a gentle slope; and the garden I am describing was so constructed that two streams of crystal-like water met in front of the building and formed an immense lake, on the surface of which numerous swans, geese, and ducks disported themselves.

Below this lake there were seven waterfalls, just as there are seven planets; and below these again there was a second lake of smaller dimensions, and a superb gateway decorated with blue tiles.

Perhaps the reader may think that this was all; but no, not only in the lakes, but also between the waterfalls, jets of water spouted up into the air so high that the falling spray resembled masses of diamonds. And often, when reclining in the beautiful tiled room, the plash of the jets of water and the murmur of the stream hurrying down the terraced garden between rose bushes, backed by weeping willows, planes, acacias, cypresses, and every other description of tree, have moved me strangely; and I have wept from pure joy, and have then been lulled to sleep by the overpowering sense of beauty and the murmur of the running water. By Allah! I think, indeed, that this garden is not surpassed in beauty by even that famous garden mentioned in the Koran:

The garden of Iram, adorned with lofty pillars:
The like of which had not been created in the world.

THE GARDEN AT MAHUN

On the appointed day, one hour before noon, my father, his chief officers and myself, duly met the Vakil-ul-Mulk at the main gate. His Excellency was in a truly good humour, and, in reply to my father's welcome and assurance that "the garden was a gift to him," replied that he regarded him as his own son. To this my father, with proud humility, answered "I am a slave born in your family." His Excellency next said that he had heard a good report of me, which made me hang my head from modesty.

Accompanied by the nobles, the Vakil-ul-Mulk walked along the edge of the lake with great dignity and very slowly, for, in Persia, only Europeans and men of low extraction walk quickly. He then ordered some bread to be brought, and fed the swans for quite a long time, while we stood waiting in attendance.

At length His Excellency entered the chief room alone, and we all stood respectfully outside by the open windows.

Opposite the cushions, on which the Vakil-ul-Mulk reclined, were two large trays full of sweetmeats prepared in the women's apartments. Among these were toffee, almond paste, "elephant's ears" in pastry, burnt almonds, sugar drawn as fine as hair, and many other delicious sweetmeats which are only made in Iran. There was also a box of manna from Isfahan. Between the trays of sweetmeats was a silver tray, on which was spread an exquisitely fine shawl, worth at least two hundred tomans [1]; and on the shawl was a sealed packet, containing two hundred ashrafis or gold pieces.

The Vakil-ul-Mulk tasted the sweetmeats, and, looking at the jets of water shining in the sun and the lovely garden, repeated:

If there is a Paradise on the face of the earth:
It is this, it is this, it is this.

His Excellency then invited his Vizier and my father to enter by a nod of the head; and, in the same manner, he dismissed the nobles and his attendants, who were shown by me to the different rooms prepared for them, as the chief servants all have their separate staffs, and so have to sit in separate rooms.

The Vakil-ul-Mulk again tasted the sweetmeats, and especially praised the toffee and also the manna which, with quails, formed the food of the Beni Israel [2] during the forty years they wandered in the deserts; and my father bowed low to express his gratitude.

Tea was then served, and the special water pipe of the Vakil-ul-Mulk, of beaten gold studded with turquoises, for which Iran is famous, was brought in.

After pulling at it in silence for a minute, His Excellency inquired from his chief waiter where he had procured such excellent tobacco; and that official replied that it was given by my father who, to grace the auspicious occasion, had bought up a stock that had reached Kerman on the previous day from Shiraz. He added that my father had supplied a large quantity of this tobacco if he might accept it. His Excellency said it was not needed; but

---

[1] A toman is worth four shillings and a kran is one-tenth of a toman.
[2] Sc. the children of Israel.

finally accepted the gift, and my father afterwards gave the servant a handsome sum of money for his friendly behaviour.

After a while, my father represented that luncheon was ready to be served, and went into the adjoining room to superintend the spreading of the table-cloth, which is made of red Hamadan leather and covered with chintz.

The waiters of the Vakil-ul-Mulk, however, declined to spread the cloth without orders from the chief of the Private Apartments, who equally declined to pay any attention until the whispered promise of a gift made him energy personified.

On the edge of the cloth twelve flat loaves of very white flour were placed; and there were huge trays of plain rice boiled as only it is boiled in Persia, with the savoury browned parts, flanked by other mounds of rice, in which the flesh of lambs and chickens with raisins, almonds, and saffron were all skilfully blended.

The bowls of broth, the dishes of meat cooked in pomegranate or lime juice, or with walnuts, were smaller, and were placed in an outer line, together with cheese, curds, vegetables, and preserved fruits.

At length all was ready, down to the priceless china bowls of sherbet, in which floated the translucent spoons of Abadeh in a mass of crushed ice, sherbet alone being drunk in public; and the Vakil-ul-Mulk, on being informed that the luncheon was served, rose from his cushion and, walking to the next room, seated himself in the place of honour.

After having partaken of some food with a good appetite, His Excellency gave orders that the Vizier and my father should be sent for. They appeared, bowed low, and were honoured by being invited to join the Governor-General, whereupon they sat down very respectfully in the lowest place. This was, in truth, a great distinction for my father, as His Excellency always sat down alone to meals, not even permitting his sons to partake of food in his presence.

Kabobs of gazelle were brought in, wrapped up in a piece of bread to keep them hot; and His Excellency said that it was not necessary to ask who lead shot it.

The repast was eaten almost in silence; and so large were the mounds of food that they seemed almost intact when, after tasting a Natanz pear preserved in syrup, and praising its flavour, the Vakil-ul-Mulk called for the jug and basin, with which he washed his hands and beard, for you must know that we Persians not only sit on our knees, but, like the Prophet, on Him be Peace, eat with our fingers, rolling together our rice into balls and then inserting them with our thumbs into the mouth.

In later years I once saw an English officer try to do this, but we all agreed that he ate just like a tiger, and that only Persians could eat, in this fashion, in a refined manner; also we know by experience that food eaten with the hand is of a better flavour, and that it is impossible to satisfy the appetite if knife and fork be used.

After this the Vakil-ul-Mulk retired with his most confidential servant for a siesta, and then, and not until then, was the sealed packet of gold coins opened and the shawl examined. His Excellency reclined on a cushion embroidered with pearls, on which was placed a large pillow and a second very small one, stuffed with swan's down, brought from the province of Sistan. A thin silk coverlet kept off the flies.

The confidential servant, when his master had composed himself to sleep, went out, gently closed the door, and lay down outside ready to be in attendance when summoned.

In less than an hour a cough announced the awakening of the Governor-General, who again washed his hands and face, and carefully combed his majestic beard, his moustaches, his eyebrows, and even his black eyelashes. He then arose, proceeded to the chief room, and, sending for the Khans and his attendants, said that, as it was too hot to go outside, he wished every one to sit down. After this he ordered tea to be served.

The conversation turned on allusion, in which Persians excel, and the Vakil-ul-Mulk himself, who was in a remarkably good humour, and did not order a single servant to eat sticks that day, told us of how Mahmud of Ghazni requited Firdausi, the author of the greatest poem in the world, so inadequately, that the poet wrote a famous satire on him which runs:

Long years this Shahnama I toiled to complete,

That the King might award me some recompense meet,
But naught save a heart wrung with grief and despair
Did I get from those promises empty as air!
Had the sire of the King been some Prince of renown,
My forehead had surely been graced by a crown!
Were his mother a lady of high pedigree,
In silver and gold had I stood to the knee!
But, being by birth not a prince but a boor,
The praise of the noble he could not endure!

Fearing retribution, Firdausi wisely fled some days before the satire was delivered, and ultimately took refuge with the Sipahbud of Tabaristan, who was the only prince of Persian descent reigning in Persia, which was then unhappily divided into separate principalities.

Sultan Mahmud was so furious when he read the satire that he fainted from excess of anger. He then sent messengers with copies of the poet's portrait to every court to inquire whether Firdausi was there, and on finding that he had taken refuge in Tabaristan, he wrote to the Sipahbud demanding the surrender of the poet, and ended his letter by threatening that, if his desire were not complied with, he would come with his war elephants and trample the country beneath their feet.

SHAYKH SINAN MEETS THE CHRISTIAN MAIDEN.
From the collection of Major Sykes.

The Sipahbud, who was prepared to defend his guest to the death, sent back the Sultan's letter and merely wrote "Alm" on the back. Mahmud was too ignorant to understand what this meant and was utterly amazed; but one of his Persian courtiers at once explained that by "Alm" the Sipahbud intended to remind the Sultan of the fate of Abraha the Abyssinian, who, also relying on war elephants, invaded Mecca in the very year of the Prophet's birth; but Allah the All-wise did he not cause flocks of birds to pelt them with pellets of baked clay so that they were discomforted? He added that the "Chapter of the Elephant" began with "Alm." When Sultan Mahmud understood this matter he trembled, and his threat remained unfulfilled.

For a long while every one was silent, and then the conversation turned to the politeness of Persians, and Husein Ali Khan said that when he was an attendant at the foot of the throne of Mohamed Shah there was a great dispute with the Minister of France because the Governor of Shiraz had, so he averred, seized a large sum of money, twenty thousand tomans, belonging to a French merchant, whereas that trustworthy official explained that he had merely taken charge of it to save it from Kashgai robbers.

In any case, at the fête in honour of the birth of the Shah, when the Chief Vizier gave a banquet, the Minister refused to be among the guests unless this sum were paid; and this abstention being reported to Mohamed Shah, that exalted monarch was displeased.

Finally, the noble Vizier not only paid the money from his private purse, but, greeting the Minister of France with exquisite urbanity, he said: "Your Excellency, this banquet has cost me twenty thousand tomans; but I would gladly have paid double the sum for the pleasure of entertaining the Minister of France." Hearing this, we felt that it was in Persia alone that such noble, high-souled ministers were born; and we all thanked Allah that we were Iranis.

The Commander-in-Chief then said that, not only in allusion and in politeness were Persians far ahead of all other nations, but that in astuteness there was no other people even second to them.

In proof of this, he told us that on one occasion he had to pay his regiment about ten tomans a man; but, owing to his misfortunes, he had only a hundred tomans instead of the necessary five thousand. However, astuteness came to his aid, and he paid every man his due, made him seal his receipt, and then, as he passed into an outer room, the money was taken from him and returned. In short, after paying away five thousand tomans, he had still a hundred tomans left. At hearing this every one laughed, and the Vakil-ul-Mulk called the Commander-in-Chief a blackguard; but only in jest.

SHAYKH AHMAD

Shaykh Ahmad then said that he knew of yet another story connected with Sultan Mahmud, who, the son of a slave, rose to be a mighty monarch and thirsted for a title from the Caliph. He sent a large gift to the Caliph, but nothing for his Vizier, who was, of course, a Persian, and who, in drawing up the order, gave instructions that Mir should be written instead of Amir.

Now Mir means a chief, but also a slave; so Mahmud was furious at this insult, until a Persian courtier explained to him that the "A"[1] which was omitted conveyed a delicate hint that he had not sent one thousand gold coins to the Vizier; but that, if the order were returned with that sum, no doubt apologies would be made and a fresh order, written as His Majesty desired, would be sent. And so, by Allah, it turned out; and thus was Sultan Mahmud educated by clever Iranis.

Abu Turab Khan represented that he could give a case which had happened only a few years ago at the court of the Vakil-ul-Mulk, but that he would not dare to mention it without permission. His Excellency was very curious to hear the story, and agreed to pardon the Khan, who said that, three years ago, a Tehran merchant came down to examine into the accounts of his agent, who had been in charge of his land for ten years and who had embezzled thousands of tomans.

But this agent was very clever, and so he paid the chief executioner two hundred tomans to come secretly to the Tehrani the morning after his arrival, and whisper in his ear that orders had just come by telegram to the Vakil-ul-Mulk for him to be thrown into chains and sent back to Tehran.

This so alarmed Aga Hadi that he too paid the chief executioner two hundred tomans and, mounting his horse, he rode off and never returned to Kerman!

Hearing this, the Vakil-ul-Mulk rolled on the ground, helpless with laughter. He then called for the chief executioner and asked him if this were true, and finally it was acknowledged.

"Blackguard," screamed the Vakil-ul-Mulk, and again rolled over.

"By Allah!" quoth he, "how fast Aga Hadi must have ridden, and how tired such a fat man as he is must have been!"

It was now two hours to sunset, and His Excellency exclaimed, "Bismillala! let us go." Everything was in a tumult, all the chief servants shouting out their orders; but by the time His Excellency had walked slowly past the lake to the great gate, his carriage was ready, guarded by three hundred

---

[1] Alif or A signifies one thousand.

sowars; and, preceded by mounted attendants bearing silver maces, who shouted out to clear the road, the stately cortège disappeared in a cloud of dust on the road to Kerman.

FROM AN OLD TILE

AN AWFUL TRAGEDY

FROM A BRONZE MIRROR

> And Bahrain, that great Hunter—the wild Ass
> Stamps o'er his Head, but cannot break his Sleep.
> Omar Khayyam.

MY father was renowned as a hunter even in Iran, where hunting has been the chief pastime of its monarchs and nobles from the days of Kei Khusru [1] down to the present day. In this connection it is well known that courtiers who exhibited special courage and skill in the chase were always sure to attract the eye of favour of their monarch. I have heard it stated that "hunting is a business for the idle"; but those who really understand are aware that hundreds of secrets for the government of kingdoms are hidden in this art.

After having ruled Mahun for many years, my father was very glad to be appointed Governor of Sirjan. This district, apart from its great extent, is always entrusted to a most capable official, owing to its situation on the borders of Fars, where the tribesmen are raiders by nature and require watching by day and night.

Dividing Sirjan from Fars is a great salt swamp which is very dangerous, except to those who know it well; but as it is also a favourite haunt of the gazelle and of the wild ass, my father was perhaps more pleased at that fact than at anything else, little knowing that Hafiz prophesied truly in his case when he wrote:

---

[1] Persians, quite incorrectly, believe that Kei Khusru was Cyrus the Great. Actually he belongs to Indo-Persian legend.

This far-off desert is the stage,
In which the armies of Salm and Tur disappeared.

I well recollect the journey to Saiidabad, the capital, over a high range where we rode in every direction in search of partridges. Our sowars spread out on each side of the track for a, farsakh, and, as partridges only fly a short distance, they were shot in large numbers or seized by falcons, of which His Excellency kept a large number. To see the intrepidity with which the sowars galloped up and down steep mountains and shot hares and even partridges at full speed would prove to any one that the Persian sowar has no equal.

On the borders of Sirjan, many of the leading Khans met us, and at Saiidabad the reception party included every one in the capital, from the great landowners and merchants to the beggars and little children.

The house of the Governor was very large with a fine garden; but it was in such a dilapidated condition that, at first, we lived in tents in the garden while it was being prepared for our reception: indeed, I recollect my fatherv stating that he had to spend a large sum on repairing it.

A few weeks after our arrival it was decided to go on a shooting expedition; and I was allowed to join the party on a well-trained horse. As soon as we were clear of the town and had reached the open country, our sowars spread out, two and two, leaving an interval of about five hundred yards between each couple, until the whole plain was covered. In the centre my father, Aga Ali, his chief gunbearer, and myself rode, and, on both sides of us, the line of sowars was slightly thrown forward like a crescent moon.

We proceeded slowly in this manner for perhaps a farsakh, when suddenly Aga Ali whose eyes were like those of a hawk, espied a herd of seven gazelles which were grazing a long way ahead of us. When they, in time, sighted us they threw up their heads and galloped off, while we continued on exactly as before.

THE GOVERNOR'S FALCONS

This went on for half a hour when, suddenly, the gazelles, which do not like leaving their grazing ground, stopped, turned round, and galloped between my father and Mohamed Mehdi Khan, who was on his left. At first the two groups moved slowly on inclining inwards; but, when it was clear that the gazelles had made up their minds and were flying like the wind, both parties galloped to cut them off. So successful were they that the gazelles passed within fifteen yards of my father who, with his number ten gun, loaded with slugs, shot two of them.

Imitating him, by throwing my reins on to the neck of my horse, I also shot a gazelle, which much pleased my father, who shouted, "Thanks be to Allah! The lion's whelp will be like its sire." I was so elated at hearing this from my father, who scarcely ever spoke to me, that my head turned round. Aga Ali, too, who had taught me to throw down my reins and to always turn in the saddle when shooting, a feat no European has ever learned, paid my father many compliments, and was promised a gift of a hundred tomans. Such a Hatim Tai [1] was my sire!

---

[1] Hatim Tai is the example in the East of a generous Arab chieftain. On one occasion having no food, he slew his famous mare to satisfy the hunger of a guest.

That night we camped near the swamp, and as sixteen gazelles had been shot, every one was much elated, and, round the fires, the ramrods of the rifles were covered with meat: indeed, Allah knows, I never tasted such delicious meat as that of the gazelle roasted in this fashion.

Early next morning we started off to hunt the wild ass along the swamp, and both my father and myself took our rifles instead of our number ten guns. Now, you must know that the wild ass is easier to approach than the gazelle, if the swamp is hard enough for a horse to gallop on it, but yet soft enough for the hoofs of the wild ass, which are much smaller, to break through.

We rode along as on the previous day, and, very soon after leaving camp, Aga Ali was the first to sight a large herd of wild asses, who galloped off and then circled back to look at us, so curious are they. This they did three times and then tried to break through; but they were turned towards the swamp, and soon sank in so much that we were able to ride up alongside them and shoot them quite easily; in fact our rifles nearly touched them as we fired.

THE "WHITE FORT"

That night again every one was very happy, as the flesh of the wild ass is esteemed a great delicacy; but, in my opinion, nothing is more delicate than the flesh of the gazelle.

On another occasion we set out hawking, and when riding along, we saw an extraordinary white rock, shaped like an egg, rise out of the plain. My father asked Mohamed Mehdi Khan what it was, as he was learned in these questions; and he replied that, on this rock, known as "White Fort," were the ruins of a famous fortress, which was once the capital of the province of Kerman. He added that it was a great show place and that there were many sand partridges there. Moved by the hope of shikar my father said, "Bismillah, let us see this wonderful place."

H. R. Sykes, phot.

THE STONE PULPIT OF THE " WHITE FORT "
(Dated A.D. 1387)

We rode to the rock and found the whole plain covered with the ruins of a mighty city. In one place was a beautiful pulpit of white stone; but everything else was in ruins. Riding up the steep white rock we found the remains of palaces, and also visited a great cave on the north side where the women, according to tradition, spent the heat of the day.

Mohamed Mehdi Khan showed us every corner, and said that Amir Timur's troops besieged the fort for three years, and then only captured it because the garrison had no supplies left, so strong was this fort. He added that, in memory of this siege, one of the hills, which he pointed out, is termed "The Throne of Timur" to this day.

Two years were spent at Saiidabad in this fashion, hunting parties being so frequent that at last the game was almost all killed. During this period the robbers from Fars never raided into Sirjan from fear of my father, and also because they were ruled by a stern Governor-General, who, whenever he caught a brigand, "plastered"[1] him up as a terrible warning to his fellows.

However, this stern ruler was dismissed, and his successor was so noted for his kindness of disposition, that, even before he reached Shiraz, the Lashanis prepared to raid Sirjan.

Owing to the fact that there had been no trouble for so many years, there was no watch kept, and we first realised what was occurring by seeing villages burning in the hills to the north of the capital just before sunset. As soon as this was noticed my father's face became terrible, and he swore that he would cut off the robbers and deal with them as the Governor-General of Fars had done.

Well do I recollect the excitement and confusion which first occurred; but yet, within half-an-hour, the whole party of two hundred sowars was ready to start. We moved at an amble, which pace is best for horses going a long distance, and when dawn broke we were approaching the main route across the morass. Upon reaching it, Aga Ali, who was famous for tracking, pointed out that about sixty horsemen had passed eastwards just a day before, but that there were no return tracks. However, he also pointed out that, as the swamp was dry at this season of the year, a second track across it to the north might well be used by the Lashanis on their return.

This much disturbed my father, who had felt sure of cutting off the raiders; and so he consulted for an hour while the horses were being fed, and we all

---

[1] Robbers are embedded in plaster up to their shoulders. When it dries up, it contracts, and their sufferings are terrible; but, if given food and water, they frequently linger on for three or four days.

lay in ambush in a grove of tamarisks, hoping for the return of the raiders who, however, never came.

It was finally settled by His Excellency, that he would take eighty of the best men and ride north so as to hold the second track; and I was left with Aga Ali in charge of the main body.

For the remainder of that day and the next we watched all in vain, until Aga Ali swore that the Lashanis had escaped, when, in the distance, we sighted one of our sowars, who rode up to me like a whirlwind, crying He then fell off his horse in a faint.

Dust on my head,
The Master is dead.

At last he was able to tell his mournful tale, which was that my father and his party were approaching the northern track across the swamp, when they saw the Lashanis already on it, driving away cattle, sheep, and other plunder.

Furious at this, and throwing prudence to the winds, my father rode straight across the morass to cut them off One by one his sowars were left behind; but my father pressed on until, just as he was near the track, his horse was engulfed in the bog.

He made every effort to escape; but, mad with fear, the brute seized him with its teeth, tore him from the saddle, and threw him under its hoofs; so that when, at last, two of the sowars came up, ready to help, there was only one, arm of my father remaining above the ooze, and the mad horse's head was sinking out of sight! Allah knows that I shall never forget the misery of that period, nor how my mother beat her head until she fell senseless, lamenting: Time, however, is the great teacher, and after a few days it was possible to look at the matter more calmly, and to feel some comfort and even pride in the thought that my father, a great hunter, when pursuing a nobler quarry than the wild ass, had met the same fate as the great hunter King, of whom Omar Khayyam wrote:

A thousand boats have gone down into this whirlpool:
And not a plank from them has reached the shore.

A PERSIAN SALT SWAMP

As man in this land of thorns
Reaps nothing but trouble and anxiety:
Happy is he who leaves this world quickly,
Or he who never enters it at all.

Bahram, who, all his life, was capturing wild asses (Gur):
See how the grave (Gur) has captured Bahram. [1]

I have not hitherto referred to my uncle, Mirza Hasan Khan, who, by the kindness of the Vakil-ul-Mulk, may Allah keep cool his grave, was made a Mustaufi or Revenue Official in the Kerman province. Now my uncle was married, but Allah had not blessed his tree of hope with fruit; and perhaps it was on this account that he showed such kindness to the orphan, whose lot is frequently a hard one, as Shaykh Sadi writes:—

Protect thou the orphan whose father is dead;
Brush the mud from his dress, ward all hurt from his head:

---

[1] This is the literal translation of FitzGerald's lines as given in the heading to this chapter. There is a play on Gur, which signifies a wild ass and also the grave. The monarch was known as Bahram Gur.

Thou know'st not how hard his condition must be;
When the root has been cut, is there life in the tree?
O see that he weep not, for surely God's throne
Doth quake at the orphan's most pitiful moan!

In short, my uncle was like an angel of benevolence to me, and, as soon as the heartrending news reached Kerman, heedless of hunger and sleep, he rode down post to Saiidabad, and thereby ensured that the revenue my father had to collect was duly paid in.

Moreover, he discharged all our debts and brought us to Kerman to his own house, and placed us under the shadow of his kindness.

Do thou a kind act and throw it in the Tigris,
And Allah will return it to thee in the desert.

Like our illustrious ancestor, Haji Abul Hasan Khan, my father had always displayed liberality and generosity; and my uncle found that, after paying up all we owed, nothing was left for me:

It is better that a man leave a good name behind:
Than to bequeath a decorated house.

Fortunately, my mother had received as a dowry one-third of the village of Sar Asiab, which sufficed for her wants, and I felt that I was quite able to earn my living; but exactly, in what manner, I did not know, as you cannot turn a knowledge of history and the capacity of a poet into a shoe and a hat.

However, the day after our arrival at Kerman, my uncle spoke very kindly to me, and said that he regarded me as his son, and had decided to make me his assistant in the revenue department, and, on the following day, I accompanied him to the Revenue Office of Kerman.

This most important department, on which the whole Government depends, was brought to the greatest perfection in Persia nearly a thousand years ago, by that great man, the Nizam-ul-Mulk, Vizier of Malik Shah, whose system is still in force to-day. Indeed, it is so perfect that no one except a Mustaufi can fully understand it: and, as a result, the power and wealth of revenue officials is very great. Indeed their power is, in some respects, above that of the local Governors, for when these latter came to Kerman to settle their revenue accounts, the Mustaufi in charge of each district was able to make all sorts of claims, and, as he had to give a certificate that the revenue had been paid in full, much bargaining went on until a sum was agreed upon, and then only was the certificate granted.

To resume, I found the office to consist of a large room with beautiful carpets, where all the Mustaufis sat together, and apparently drank tea, smoked, and did nothing else. However, in this I was mistaken, for every now and then a youth whispered into the ear of one of them, who thereupon gave a whispered reply. This, as I soon found out, meant that a local Governor had made an offer to the Mustaufi through his assistant, who had come to report.

Shortly after I had taken up my post, I was approached by the confidential servant of the Governor of Jiruft, who offered six hundred tomans for his certificate, accompanied by many compliments to myself. This I reported to my uncle, who remarked smilingly, "Lessen the compliments and increase the money," and said that I was to reply that one thousand tomans was the lowest sum he would accept. For a week this bargaining went on and, at last, eight hundred tomans were paid, and also a present of fifty tomans to myself, about which I did not say anything to my uncle, as that was my perquisite.

As I found that the revenue officials were all people of a noble disposition, who evinced much respect for my uncle, I soon became very happy at Kerman. Indeed, I found that I was able not only to master all the intricacies of the revenue system of Persia, but also to continue to study poetry, history, and geography. In short, I attained contentment, and as Shaykh Sadi writes:

O soul! if thou acquirest contentment,
Thou wilt exercise sway in the kingdom of repose.

FROM AN OLD VASE

MY BETROTHAL AND MARRIAGE

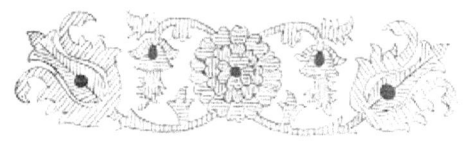

Now when once more the Night's ambrosial dusk
Upon the skirts of Day had poured its musk,
In sleep an angel caused him to behold
The heavenly gardens' radiancy untold,
Whose wide expanse, shadowed by lofty trees,
Was cheerful as the heart fulfilled of ease.
Each flow'ret in itself a garden seemed,
Each rosy petal like a lantern gleamed.
Each glade reflects, like some sky-scanning eye,
A heavenly mansion from the azure sky.
Like brightest emeralds its grasses grow,
While its effulgence doth no limit know.
Goblet in hand, each blossom of the dale
Drinks to the music of the nightingale.
Celestial harps melodious songs upraise,
While cooing ring-doves utter hymns of praise.
                Nizami's Laila and Majnun

One day my uncle spoke to me with great kindness, and said that, as I was fully eighteen years of age, it was time that I thought of marriage. He then advised me not to prize beauty alone; but rather to hope for a modest, pious, capable woman, who would speak little, but who would be economical, discreet, and prudent. "If thou marriest such a woman," he cried, "she will be the prop and stay of thy existence."

On the other hand, said he, as Shaykh Sadi wrote:

A bad woman in the house of a virtuous man is his hell, even in this world. Save us, O Lord, from this fiery trial!

My uncle finally quoted from the Sayings of the Prophet, "Second only to the benefit of believing the faith of Islam, is that of marrying a Mussulman wife, who rejoices the eyes of a man, obeys his wishes, and, during his absence, watches faithfully over his house and possessions."

Upon hearing these words I was deeply moved, and was only able to reply: I then went off to the women's apartments, where my mother greeted me with a significant smile; and I soon understood that she had been the instigator in this plot and that she had already been busy for some time in arranging a marriage for me.

What objection can a servant raise?
It is for the Master to command.

You do not perhaps know that, when a mother considers it time for her son to marry, she makes inquiries in every direction, by means of special agents who are generally old women, and when they hear of a girl who is handsome, of a docile disposition, and of suitable family, she and a friend call upon her mother, who, when the subject is first broached, makes excuses, such as that the girl has been dedicated to a Sayyid. [1]

This, however, is merely to show that there is no undue haste, and, when the girl is asked to bring sugar and water, the object of the visit is formally announced. The girl retires, adorns herself, and then brings in water, which she presents to the visitors, who embrace her and examine her very closely.

A long consultation, in which the girl has no part, now takes place, and all details are given on both sides, with much exaggeration, as to the character, qualities, and position of both the young people; and the meeting is finally brought to a close by sweetmeats being handed round.

After this, ingenuity is exercised by the women to gain a view of the proposed bridegroom, which is not difficult, as he can easily be seen riding or walking. For the youth to see his future bride is, however, quite

---

[1] If a girl be dangerously ill, her parents frequently vow that, should she recover, they will marry her to a Sayyid; or if, at first they have been disappointed in their hopes of children, a similar vow is made.

incorrect; but yet my mother had even arranged this. She had, after the first meeting, discussed the matter with her relations and friends, who knew both families and had again visited the house, and asked for sweetmeats, which is tantamount to stating that her side had agreed to the match. She also had arranged for a return visit to be paid by the girl's mother and my future bride, whose very name Shirin expressed sweetness, but who was ignorant of what was being settled.

One day my mother informed me that they would pay their visit that afternoon, and that the girl would be seated in the lowest place in the party opposite the door. She added, "If you were to look into the room through a chink at that time, remember it would be most improper, and I should speak severely to you if I saw you." My mother again smiled and, as I understood her meaning, my emotions were so overpowering that I almost fainted.

Allah knows what trouble I gave at the bath that day and how carefully I donned my best clothes, and how rakishly I placed a new kolah [1] on my head; but, even so, I was ready long before the ladies came, and in my lovesick condition I kept repeating "Shirin! Shirin!"

Say nought of the lusciousness candy contains, e'en sugar unmentioned may be;
For all, save the sugar possessed by thy lips, is wanting in savour to me.

At last, two hours before sunset, I saw from my hiding-place five ladies arrive. The leading one was, I felt sure, my future mother-in-law, who, I had been told, would be accompanied by her sister. Then came a form which, in spite of the dark blue outer robe and white veil, I saw was like a cypress, with the gait of a pheasant; and my heart revealed to me that it was my beloved. Two confidential female servants completed the party.

I knew that if I looked into the room too I soon the ladies would not have removed their outer robes or veils; so I contained myself for a quarter of an hour, although it seemed to me like a year.

---

[1] The becoming head-gear of Persia is made of the skin of the unborn lamb, and costs about £4 if of good quality.

At last, trembling like a willow branch, I quickly entered the women's apartments, and, hardly knowing what I did, instead of looking through the chink, I opened the door. As I did so, I met for one second the gaze of a houri with eyes like those of a gazelle, under eyebrows resembling a crescent moon. More than this I saw not, as a cry was raised and my beloved wrapped her robe round her and fled out of the room.

My mother and the other ladies then asked me how I dared to enter an assembly of women, and I stood abashed for a minute and then shut the door, and as if in a dream retired to my room where my heart, wounded by the darts from those eyes, kept me awake for the whole night, crying and tossing from side to side.

Tell sleep not to enter my eyes any more,
Because the island which was thy abode has been submerged in water.

However, my mother and uncle were, all the time, working in my interests, and informed me that they had agreed that the bride should be given one-sixth of the village of Sar Asiab and one thousand tomans as a dowry, half of which was to be paid in cash before and half after the marriage; also an agreement was made that the bride should never leave Kerman against her will. Indeed, the details of the agreement were so numerous that I cannot describe them.

A few weeks later the betrothal took place. In the morning six large trays containing a fine Kerman shawl, a ring set with diamonds, a pair of gold earrings and much sugar, tea, and sweetmeats were sent to the bride's house. My Shirin was then adorned and the earrings were placed in her ears by a lady of distinction, who was blessed with a family of eighteen children, of whom fourteen were sons. General rejoicings then ensued, which, however, only the ladies of both families attended; and it may be understood how I yearned for the marriage to take place, although I now understand fully that such an important event should be carried out with due delay so as to enhance the dignity of the proceedings.

Then, however, I was, I fear, ill-tempered and peevish, and could only compose verses which I thought poor, but which are now held to be worth ten gold pieces a line, such as

O Spring Cloud, discharge abundantly in the vineyard;

If a drop of rain become wine why should it be wasted in forming a pearl? [1]
Or again my famous verse, in which the four elements are mentioned:

When the morning breeze lifted the veil from thy face,
It smote to the earth the honour possessed by the fire of Zoroaster. [2]

Two months after the engagement the chief astrologer was called into consultation as to the auspicious day for the performance of the marriage ceremony; and, having fixed upon three hours to sunset on the following Wednesday, intimation to this effect was sent to the father of the bride.

On the day, a tray containing one hundred different varieties of drugs and herbs, with a mirror and ten yards of white sheeting to cover the bride during the ceremony, was sent to her home. The other gifts were two candlesticks, twenty pairs of shoes, and several trays containing sweetmeats. All these matters are regulated by etiquette, so polished and civilised a people are we Persians.

Four hours before sunset, after spending the day at the hammam, during which time my hair and nails were beautifully dyed, we assembled in the great hall at the house of Ali Naki Khan, my future father-in-law, and were greeted by the relations of both families, the ladies, meanwhile, assembling in the women's apartments.

Shirin, who on the previous day had visited the bath, had been, as she afterwards told me, placed on a saddle facing towards Mecca, with all her garments untied, until the ceremony was completed Opposite my beloved were the mirror and the comb; and, in front of the mirror, the two candlesticks were placed and lighted. The white sheet was draped over her head, and, when she was arrayed in all her wedding garments, my mother said that she resembled Bilkis, that queen of Sheba who visited Solomon the son of David.

---

[1] The Oriental believes that pearls are formed by the crystallization of drops of rain falling on the oyster.
[2] Abru is literally "water of the face," and thus the wind, the earth, water, and fire are all included.
The first verse is by Danish, Meshedi, who received 100,000 rupees as a reward from the son of Shah Jahan, the Moghul Emperor. Our author would reply to a charge of plagiarism that both he and Danish, by chance, had the same beautiful idea. This is termed Tavarud or coincidence.

Meanwhile her mouth was filled with sweetmeats, and sugar dust was sprinkled over her head by rubbing two pieces together. To increase her good fortune, a lady took a needle, threaded it with a thread made of seven coloured strands, and passed and repassed it through the white sheet which was draped over the head of the bride. This very ancient custom is never omitted. Finally, drugs were thrown into the fire until the atmosphere itself became amorous.

A PERSIAN WEDDING

The chief priest of Kerman, Aga Mohamed, who was related to my mother, performed the ceremony. When he took his seat among us, he called me to his presence and asked me if I authorised him to act as my agent. On receiving my reply in the affirmative, he inquired who was the agent on behalf of Shirin, and on hearing that it was Shaykh Abdulla he had the draft of the marriage deed, containing all the conditions, read out three times.

Shaykh Abdulla thereupon proceeded to the curtained door of the women's apartments when, on his announcing his errand, Shirin, who required much encouragement before she would speak, stated three times that she agreed to the marriage. After this, he returned and informed Aga Mohamed that Shirin had agreed to the marriage. Upon hearing this, the marriage was declared to have taken place; and congratulations were offered by all those present.

At the termination of this ceremony I was taken to the women's apartments, into the room where Shirin was sitting. She rose up to receive me and, as soon as I had placed nay hand on her head as a token of my protection to her in the future, she tried to place her foot on mine; but I, dexterously avoiding it, gently placed my foot on her foot. This ceremony is necessary, and whoever of the two places his or her foot on the foot of the other, will, we believe, continue to rule for life.

We both saw the faces of each other reflected in the mirror, which had been placed in front of Shirin; but I had to give her a handsome present in the shape of a pearl ring before I could secure to myself the pleasure of seeing her face in the mirror. It may be mentioned that, during the performance of this ceremony, all widows or twice married women, and all unmarried girls, are rigidly excluded from among the ladies sitting round the bride, as their presence is sure to bring bad luck to her.

Soon after the conclusion of the marriage ceremony I grew impatient, and began to trouble my mother with hints that the wedding should take place without delay; but she put me off by saying that the ornaments and other wedding furniture had not yet been completed by the bride's parents, who had asked for a period of at least two months for these preparations.

Allah knows how I counted the days and nights; and the moment that this period had elapsed, I again had it conveyed to my mother that she should hasten on the wedding; and I represented that, unless she wished me to become as thin as Majnun, [1] the famous lover, whom even the wild beasts pitied, she must use all her influence and not allow unnecessary delay:

The nearer the time of meeting with the beloved approaches,
The fiercer burns the flame of love.

After declaring, for some days, that such haste was not correct, my mother understood that I was really beginning to waste away; and, fortunately, just about this time, intimation was received from Shirin's mother that all the wedding furniture had been completed. My mother at once sent again for

---

[1] Majnun wasted away for the love of the famous Laila.

the chief astrologer, and he fixed on the Friday night [1] as the most auspicious of auspicious times for the consummation of the marriage.

On the afternoon of that day the wedding gifts were sent from the bride's to my uncle's house, passing through the principal streets of the city; and men and women thronged in hundreds in the streets and on their roofs to see and admire them.

All the household furniture, such as cushions, pillows, velvet curtains embroidered in gold, lamps, candlesticks, copper and porcelain utensils, tea and coffee services, and other articles too numerous to mention, were carried on trays; and carpets and boxes of clothes belonging to the bride were borne on gaily caparisoned mules, with bells round their necks and also swinging at their sides; and, with all these things, the rooms set apart for the use of the bride were prepared for her reception.

Feasting had been the order of the day both at my uncle's house and at the house of Ali Naki Khan for several days; and I had spent part of the Thursday entertaining my friends at a hammam, which had been specially reserved for this purpose; and, after giving gifts to the bath attendants who had shampooed me and dyed my hair and nails, I stepped forth, clad in a suit which my father-in-law had presented to me. This suit included a shirt made by the hand of Shirin from the white sheet which was draped over her head when the marriage ceremony was performed.

At four hours after sunset, my uncle with our male relations and friends, proceeded to the bride's house, followed at a very short distance by all our female relations, including my mother, and preceded by lighted candles, lamps, torches, and musicians; fireworks too were let off.

The men assembled in the hall, and the ladies were seated in the women's apartments, and sherbet was served, followed by tea and water pipes. My uncle then presented the completed marriage deed, which had been written out on paper, most beautifully decorated with gold and other colours, to the bride's father who took it to show to Shirin's mother.

---

[1] According to lunar mouths the day begins at sunset. Thus Friday night, by European calculation, would be Thursday night.

Meanwhile Shirin, too, had been to the hammam, where her hair and hands and feet were dyed, and her back carefully depilated to remove all traces of hair, as it is believed that there is a hair of the Angel of Death on a woman's back which, if allowed to remain, would bring ill luck to the family. After her return to the house, she was taken to a special room where her relations dressed her in her bridal clothes and ornaments.

When the bride was ready to start, the men formed themselves into a procession which was followed by a second procession, in which was Shirin, riding on a richly caparisoned Bahrein donkey, and surrounded by ladies of both families, with the exception of her own mother, who remained behind, as also her father. The bride who, at the moment of departure from her home, received some bread, salt, and cheese in a handkerchief handed to her by her youngest brother, was preceded by a man who carried a mirror with its face towards her. On the way she was stopped several times by the ladies of her family demanding gifts, which had to be presented by some prominent members of my uncle's family.

When the bride approached our house she was made to stop, and the ladies declared that she would not move forward until I myself had appeared. In the meantime I had gone to meet her, and I soon heard the clang of instruments, the noise made by the fireworks, and the hum of many excited voices.

The ladies, upon seeing me, cried out, "We have accepted you!" They added, "You have taken great trouble." I then turned back ahead of the procession.

When the bridal party reached the entrance of the street, in order to avert the evil eye, five sheep were sacrificed by order of my uncle, and the procession passed between the carcases and the severed heads, the meat being divided between the policemen, musicians, and others.

By this time I had climbed up to the gateway, and from it I caught sight of hundreds of men bearing lamps, and finally saw my beloved pass under where I was standing into the outer court of the house. Here my uncle, welcoming leer, took her hand and led her to the chamber prepared for her. Rue was burnt in front of her, and Shirin threw a gold piece into the brazier. This too is a very ancient custom for averting the evil eye.

Shirin was then kissed by my mother, and I was conducted into the chamber, and a jug and basin were prepared when I removed the Dolagh [1] of Shirin and she removed the socks from my feet. One of the women servants poured out water and I washed the big toe of her right foot and then of her left, Shirin doing the same for me; and, when this was done, we both threw a gold piece into the basin.

After this I tried to remove the veil to see her face, but I only succeeded after making her a present of a pair of golden bracelets studded with turquoises. We gazed intently at each other's face in the great mirror, and I nearly swooned with joy to feel that, at last, Shirin was in my home.

I next started conversation by inquiring after her health, and before she uttered a word in reply I had to put a few gold coins into her mouth. The tablecloth was then spread, and we both partook of some of the bread, cheese, and salt brought by the bride; and put mouthfuls of rice into each other's mouths. At this point I presented Shirin with a necklace of Bahrein pearls, an heirloom of my great ancestor; and this gift made my bride speak freely at last, as the other ladies examined it with envy:

The beauty of my beloved is independent of my incomplete love,
Her beautiful face is not in need of rouge, colour, tattooing, or a mole.

At length our lady friends and relations all departed, and as the argent moon soared through the star-spangled sky I murmured:

'Tis a deep charm which makes the lover's flame,
Not ruby lip, nor verdant down its name:
Beauty is not the eye, look, cheek, and mole,
A thousand subtle points the heart control.

At that moment the bulbul in the rose-bushes broke out into an ecstasy of song, and its notes and the intoxicating smell of the jasmine made an earthly paradise of what was now the home of Shirin.

---

[1] Dolagh is the garment worn out of doors, combining stockings and trousers.

FROM A SASANIAN BRASS BOWL

KERMAN, THE HEART OF THE WORLD

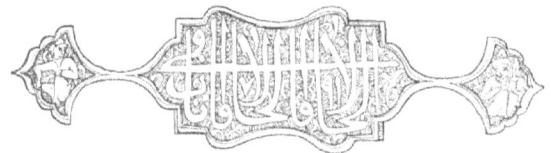

FROM AN OLD BRASS TRAY

Although we stand abashed in the presence of the noble,
It matters not, since we have drawn nourishment from this earth and water;
On the face of the earth, there is no place like Kerman;
Kerman is the heart of the world, and we are men of heart.
                                        Shah Namat Ullah.

THE origin of Kerman is famous throughout the Seven Climates, if only on account of the world-renowned legend connected with it, which I will here repeat.

In the days of Ardeshir, son of Babek, who lived many centuries before our Prophet, on him and on his descendants be peace, a maiden was spinning with her companions in a garden when she picked up an apple, within which she found a kerm or worm.

She, half in jest, vowed that if she completed her allotted task before her companions, she would cherish the worm and feed it daily. Almost at once her spinning was completed, and from that day her father's family increased in prosperity until they conquered the province, which was thenceforward known by its name of Kerman or the "Worm Province."

Ardeshir, monarch of Iran, suffered defeat after defeat at the hands of Haftan Bokht, the father of the girl, until he realised that so long as the Worm was alive he was powerless.

Consequently he resolved on a daring stratagem, and, disguising himself as a merchant prince, he presented himself before Haftan Bokht and said, that as he owed all his success in trade to the good fortune of the Worm, he requested the honour of feeding it for three days. This petition was readily granted, and as Firdausi, the greatest epic poet of all the cycles of time, writes:

When their souls were deep steeped in the wine-cup;
Forth fared the Prince with his hosts of the hamlet,
Brought with him copper and brazen cauldron,
Kindled a flaming fire in the white daylight.
So to the Worm at its meal-time was measured
In place of milk and rice much molten metal.
Unto its trench he brought that liquid copper;
Soft from the trench its head the Worm upraised.
Then they beheld its tongue, like brazen cymbal,
Thrust forth to take its food as was its custom.
Into its open jaws that molten metal
Poured he, while, in the trench, helpless the Worm writhed;
Crashed from its throat the sound of fierce explosion,
Such that the trench and whole fort fell a-quaking.
Swift as the wind Ardeshir and his comrades
Hastened with drawn swords, arrows, and maces.
Of the Worm's warders, wrapped in their wine-sleep,
Not one escaped alive from their fierce onslaught.
Then from the Castle-keep raised he the smoke-wreaths
Which his success should tell to his captains.
Hasting to Shahr-gir swift came the sentry,
Crying, "King Ardeshir his task hath finished!"
Quickly the captain then came with his squadrons,
Leading his mail-clad men unto the King's aid.

I think, O wise men of the Seven Climates, that you will agree that the origin of Kerman is out of the common, and that the city founded by Ardeshir is no ordinary city. He it was who constructed the great ditch and also the two awesome forts, reaching to the clouds, and the stronger and higher of these great fortresses still bears his name; the other is known as the "Virgin's Fort," and has never been polluted by a conqueror's triumph.

But to-day, thanks to the might of the Kajar dynasty, these forts are in ruins, as peace reigns everywhere, and the city of Kerman, which bears the illustrious title of "Abode of Safety," stretches far and wide at their feet. Not that there are no walls round the city, that would be folly; but Kerman is built on a perfect plan and has great squares, peerless mosques, and superb colleges, that make it the envy of all other cities in Persia.

The palace, too, is so magnificent that travellers consider its "Hall of Audience" to be a rival to that at the capital, but Allah knows if this be true.

No account, however, of the residence of the Governor-General would be complete without a reference to the Drum House. From the days of Jamshid, [1] who built the palaces still called by his name near Shiraz, every great city has enjoyed the privilege of hearing music, which is played from a gateway to usher in the rising sun and to play out the setting sun. Indeed, it is evident that this music is of great antiquity. The instruments consist of kettledrums of a large size, pipes, and long trumpets quite six feet long. Whenever I hear the music I feel proud that I am an Irani, whose history goes back to the days when the sun was worshipped; and even Farangis acknowledge that they have never heard any music like that of the Drum House.

E. C. Sykes, phot.

THE FORT OF ARDESHIR

---

[1] Persepolis is termed "The Throne of Jamshid" by the Persians.

Our city, compared to which Shiraz is little more than a village, is surrounded by lovely gardens, many of which are owned by the Gabrs, [1] who, although despised by all Mussulmans, are yet the best gardeners in Persia; and, after all, they are our own stock and they swear that Hazrat Ibrahim was their Prophet.

Kerman is famous for its shawls, which rival those of Kashmir, and for its carpets, which are unrivalled in the world. They say that it is the wonderful climate of the province which produces wool of such exquisite fineness; and yet, without the hereditary skill of the Kermanis, of what use would these advantages prove? Indeed, kings prize the output of the Kerman looms; and whenever a robe of honour is bestowed by the Shah, may Allah protect him! it is always a Kerman shawl of exquisite beauty and fineness. Indeed, the shawls of Kashmir, which also are very fine, are partly manufactured from Kerman wool, and so, in praising them, I also laud Kerman.

A PARSI GARDENER

---

[1] The Gabrs, or Parsis, as we term them, sometimes identify Zoroaster with Abraham. As a matter of fact, when given a chance, as in India, they prove themselves to be a very fine race. In Persia, too, they are noted for their integrity.

A PERSIAN BAND

Not that the province is without natural products, as, among many other things which grow wild for any one to collect, are the delicious caraway seeds. Indeed, so famous are they that "To take caraway seeds to Kerman" has become a proverb.

The inhabitants of my city are noted for their hospitality, and there were frequent parties in the gardens with their red roses, leafy glades, and running streams; and we spent the summer day in reciting verses or discussing the history of glorious Iran. In the winter, too, the long evenings were spent most pleasantly, as Persians, and especially the Kermanis, have so keen a wit that it is impossible to tire of listening to its sallies. In short, I thanked Allah that I had become an inhabitant of such a famous city, where my learning and wit were so fully appreciated.

A KERMAN CARPET AND ITS OWNER

Owing to the fact that the Governor-General, the Vakil-ul-Mulk, may Allah keep cool his grave! had always considered my father as one of his own family, his son, who had now succeeded him, continued to treat me with equal kindness, and I gradually became his chief courtier, and so fond was he of history and poetry that, when he went into the mountains during the "Forty days of Heat," he always took me in his service; and thus my position and wealth were increased. Indeed, I soon began to be employed on matters of importance, as will be shown later on.

I have not hitherto mentioned that in Kerman there lived an English doctor who, when he first came, was looked upon as a stranger; but, Allah knows, in surgery the English surpass even our best hakims, and, as Allah the Omnipotent used the Sahib as a medium to restore the sight of my uncle, who had a cataract in his left eye, I became a great friend of his; and indeed it was he who suggested that the inhabitants of London and of the New World would like to read the story which is now being written.

In addition to a hospital, a school was opened by the English, and to it a few of the sons of the Khans were sent. The Vakil-ul-Mulk, whose grandfather had been the official entertainer of Sir John Malcolm, when that illustrious Englishman was appointed ambassador at the foot of the throne of Fath Ali Shah, was most kind to the English; and perhaps it is not known that once when a high official asked him to name what gift the British Government should offer him, he replied that he wished a Persian translation of the ambassador's History of Persia to be made and presented to him.

I always consider that this action showed how noble was the character of the Vakil-ul-Mulk, and I shall never forget his reply to his Vizier who had represented that, in his opinion, a hundred rifles would have been a more useful gift. The Vakil-ul-Mulk simply replied, "Listen what Shaykh Sadi says:

"Sons of Adam from learning will find perfection,
Not from dignity, and rank, and wealth, and property;
Like a taper one must melt in pursuit of learning,
Since without learning one cannot know God."

Now I do not want it thought that I who am, Allah be praised, a pious Mussulman, am a lover of European ways. Far from it, I am no fool, and what I know, I know.

Once, our Governor-General sent one of his sons to Europe with plenty of money, and with instructions to study history, law, geography, all sciences and languages, and above all, Parliament.[1] Well, Fazal Ullah Khan spent several years and much money in London, and wrote to his father such accounts of his learning and of the attentions paid to him by its Viziers, who, according to him, vied with one another in honouring him, that the Governor-General was transported with delight, and frequently exclaimed in Durbar that, without the slightest doubt, Fazal Ullah Khan would, one

---

[1] The strength of the British nation is held to be derived from this word, which was formerly believed to be magical.

day, be Grand Vizier of Persia, or, if not that, he would certainly become Vizier for Foreign Affairs.

At length Fazal Ullah Khan wrote to his father that he was returning to his service, and His Excellency, who was camping in the hills during the "Forty days of Heat," gave orders for him to be met with the highest honours by all his servants, of whom I was one of the chief.

The reception party consisted of three hundred sowars under a general, but with the Governor's chief officer in supreme charge. There were also twenty mounted servants leading superb horses with collars of gold round their necks and gorgeous Resht saddle-cloths; and the Governor's favourite horse was sent for Fazal Ullah Khan to ride upon. In truth, had he been a prince more honour would not have been shown him.

Near the camp, ten servants with silver maces and sixty farrashes led the future Vizier to where His Excellency awaited him alone. Fazal Ullah Khan flung himself off his horse and wished to do obeisance to his father; but the latter, kissing him on the mouth, led him by the hand to a tent which they entered alone.

After a short silence His Excellency said, "My son, during the course of your many years of travel, tell me what is the most extraordinary thing thou hast observed." "Lord of my life," was the reply, "may I be thy ransom; but, in London, even the little boys spoke the English tongue."

The Governor made no reply, but rose and left the tent. He was immediately surrounded by the nobles of the province, who expressed hopes that he was satisfied with his son. The only reply I heard was, "My money has been burnt."

That night this matter and nothing else was under discussion, and I quoted the following verse:—

From the miracles of our spiritual Leader what a wonder!
The snow fell, and he stated "the snow is falling."

Needless to say, none of us Kermanis have, since that date, thought of educating our sons in Europe; and surely we are wiser than the Tehranis, who are now constantly sending their sons to Paris and London. There is also the fear lest our youths might become enamoured of a Christian maiden and follow the evil example of Shaykh Sinan, who, in like case, deserted his band of disciples and grazed a herd of swine. As Sadi wrote:

I saw a holy man in a mountain,
Who, abandoning the world, took up his abode in a cave;
I asked him, "Why dost thou not visit the city
So that thou mightest distract thyself somewhat?"
He replied, "There are beauteous fairies there;
When there is much mud, the elephants slip."

In short, whenever I pass the school which is held near my house and hear all the boys learning to recite our holy Koran, I exclaim, "Praise be to Allah, this is true education." Moreover, if a boy complains to me of the severity of the teacher and the frequency with which punishment is inflicted, I reply, "Know, 'O son,' that a blow from the teacher's rod is like a rose leaf." Thus do I comfort scholars.

I have not hitherto referred fully to the question of religion, and I do not expect that this work will move Christians to become true believers; but yet I know that there is much ignorance among them; and so it is right that I should lessen this by giving some account of our religion, and, to begin with, it is impossible to do better than to narrate the interview between the early refugees from Mecca and the Negus of Abyssinia.

Then the Negus sent unto the followers of the Apostle of Allah. So when they came to him, he inquired of them saying, "What is this religion, by reason of which ye have separated from your people, yet enter not withal into my religion, nor into the religion of any other of these churches?"

Then answered him Jafar, the son of Abu Talib (may the approval of Allah rest upon him!), saying, "O King! We were a barbarous folk, worshipping idols, eating carrion, committing shameful deeds, violating the ties of consanguinity, and evilly entreating our neighbours, the strong amongst us consuming the weak; and thus we continued until Allah sent unto us an Apostle from our midst, whose pedigree, and integrity, and faithfulness, and purity of life we knew, to summon us to Allah, that we should declare His unity, and worship Him, and put away the stones and idols which we and our fathers used to worship in His stead; and he bade us be truthful in speech, and faithful in the fulfilment of our trusts, and observing of the ties of consanguinity and the duties of neighbours, and to refrain from forbidden things and from blood; and he forbade us from immoral acts and deceitful words, and from consuming the property of orphans, and from slandering virtuous women; and he commanded us to worship Allah, and to associate naught else with Him, and to pray, and give alms and fast." Then the Negus wept and said to them, "Verily this and that which Moses brought emanate from one lamp."

O men of Europe, surely it is wiser for us who are "People who possess a revealed Scripture" to agree with the Negus than to remain divided as if by a bottomless gulf.

To resume, it is, of course, known to the instructed that the Mussulmans in the world are divided into two great divisions and seventy-two subdivisions. The Persians term themselves Shias or "Separatists," and the rest of the Mussulmans are, generally speaking, Sunnis or "Followers of the Traditions," although there are many Shias in Hindustan and elsewhere.

We Shias consider that Hazrat Ali, on Him and on his family be Peace, was the true successor of the Prophet. Consequently, the three caliphs who ruled before Ali came to his rights are considered to be usurpers by us; Omar, in particular, who conquered Persia, being especially accursed. It is also firmly believed that the last Imam is not dead, but hidden. Inshallah! I shall refer to this question again.

Ali is the pearl of the ocean of eternity;
Ali is the successor of Mohamed.

Apart from the great division between the Shias and Sunnis there are also minor divisions, and, in Kerman, almost all the Khans belonged to the Shaykhi sect, and believed that at the resurrection men would only arise in the spirit and not in the flesh. Moreover, it was believed that there must always be a special channel of grace between the hidden Imam and his church. Haji Mohamed Kerim Khan of the Kajar family was the head of the Shaykhis when I first lived at Kerman; and, as my mother also belonged to the Kajar family, I was brought up to respect them.

Yet it is the Sufi creed which really attracted me, and which I have already referred to. Many are the hours I spent listening to the Murshid or Spiritual Head of the Mahun Shrine, and my heart approved when he repeated again and again that all religious fanaticism was the result of ignorance, and that it must be swept away to make place for universal love.

Do not listen to the strife amongst the seventy-two religions:
Not seeing the way of reality they have strayed into romance.

During the whole of his life he slept but four hours in the night, merely wrapping himself in his brown cloak, and lying down on the bare floor. Moreover, he strictly limited himself to the number of mouthfuls of food which he deemed actually necessary to sustain his slender frame.

He died while giving a lecture to his eager disciples on the love of Allah, murmuring 'Hu, Hu, Hu.'[1] In truth he was a holy man. May Allah forgive him!

I have referred to this question, for Allah knows there be enough sinners among the Mussulmans; but they alone will travel for months across deserts, and bear heat and cold, hunger and thirst, which kills many among them. Yet on they press in thousands, and all in the hope that they may gaze on the tomb of the martyred Imam, the innocent Riza. On Him and on his family be Peace! To make this pilgrimage one day became, from this period, my fixed desire.

---

[1] Sc. He, meaning thereby God.

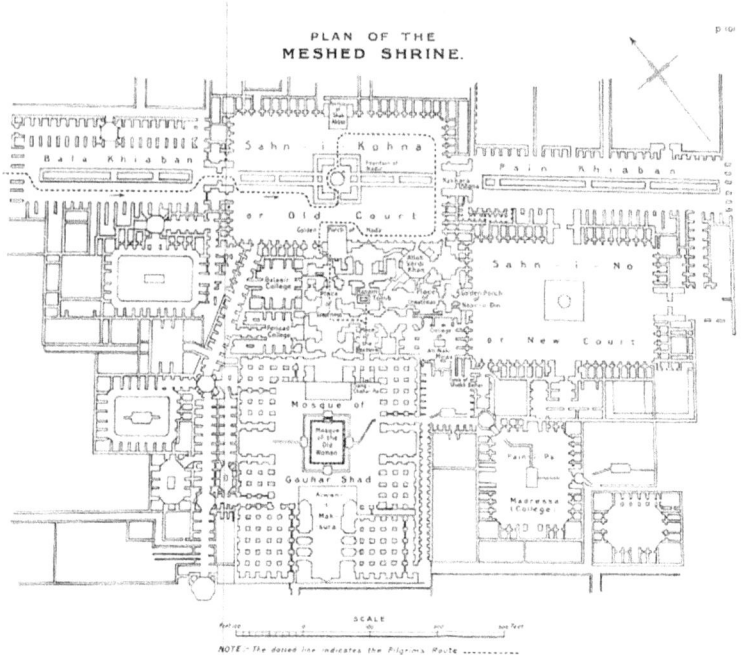

To conclude this chapter what better can I say than that—
Kerman is the heart of the world, and we are men of heart.

DESIGN FROM AN OLD BRASS TRAY

THE DEATH OF MIRZA HASAN KHAN, MUSTAUFI

FROM AN EARTHENWARE WATER PIPE

Many are the famous and many are the fortunate,
Who have rent the garment of life,
Who have drawn the head within the wall of the grave.
                Sadi.

IT was about three years after my marriage when my uncle addressed me with much solemnity and said, "Oh my son, up to the age of forty years a man develops; but after this he remains stationary, just as the sun when it has reached the meridian seems to stop, and then to move more slowly until it begins to set.

"From forty to fifty years a man feels that he is failing every year, but after reaching this age he feels it every month until he is sixty, when he feels it every week. Now I, my son, have passed seventy years, and, as the poet writes:

"Hast thou won a throne higher than the Moon;
Hast thou the power and the wealth of Solomon!
When the fruit is ripe, it falls from the tree;
When Thou hast attained thy limit, it is time to depart."

A few days after speaking these words, Mirza Hasan Khan fell ill with fever, and so Haji Mohamed Khan, the Chief Physician of the quarter, was summoned. At first he encouraged us by giving proofs of his perception, as he said to my uncle that he knew that he had partaken of fowl that day, which happened to be true; and Allah alone knows how he was aware of this, unless indeed he saw its feathers lying outside the kitchen.

The Chief Physician, after making the most minute inquiries, ordered that all pickles and all white foods, such as milk, cheese, or curds, should be given up; and he prescribed a broth of meat, vegetables, and rice all boiled together.

He added that it was most important that the meat should be cut from the neck of the sheep. Moreover, as the disease was pronounced to be of a cold type, castor oil, which is a warm drug, was administered as a purgative, followed by boiling water containing sugar.

It was expected that, on the seventh night, perspiration would set in; but as the fever was still strong, the legs of the patient were fumigated and mustard was rubbed in. Perspiration was again expected on the ninth night; but as there was no abatement in the fever a family council was held, and it was decided to call in Mirza Sadik Khan, the Chief Physician of the Vakil-ul-Mulk.

This physician was famous throughout the province for having cured a man who was at the point of death from a bone sticking in his throat, and as, perhaps, some European doctor may read this story, I advise him to note how this successor of Avicenna added lustre to the glories of Persian science.

The patient was brought in on the verge of death, and when his condition had been described, the learned physician stroked his long beard and exclaimed, "By Allah! this case would be hopeless except for me, whose perception is phenomenal. The cause of this man's state is a bone lodged in the throat so firmly that no efforts avail to dislodge it. Therefore either the man must quickly die or the bone must be dissolved, and by what agency?

"Thanks be to Allah! I am a physician and a Kermani, and have observed that wolves, who live on raw meat and bones, never suffer any calamity such as that of the patient. Therefore it is clear to me that the breath of a wolf dissolves bones, and that, if one breathes down the throat of the patient, the bone will be dissolved."

Infinite are the marvels of Allah! for when a wolf, belonging to a buffoon, was brought in and breathed on the patient, suddenly a fit of choking ensued, and the bone, dissolved without doubt by the breath of the wolf, was loosened and extracted.

Since that date the Vakil-ul-Mulk would consult no other physician, and occasionally condescended to remark that his physician was fit to rank with Plato.

However, the arrival of the Governor-General's doctor much displeased Haji Mohamed Khan, and when Mirza Sadik Khan declared the disease to be of a hot type and prescribed broth composed of the flesh of cocks which are cold, as opposed to hens which are hot, in addition to a draught of water-melon juice with melon seeds; and, finally, when he entirely forbade the use of salt, there was a great quarrel, so much so that my uncle bade them, in Allah's name, to leave him to die in peace, and to allow him to follow the path of her who is forgiven, meaning thereby his deceased wife.

He also quoted from the Koran, "Wheresoever ye be death will overtake you, although ye be in lofty towers."

At this time Izrail, the Angel of Death, was, in truth, knocking at the door; and that no one can stay his entrance, is shown by what happened in the case of the Prophet, on Him be peace!

It is recorded in the Book of Calamity, and runs as follows [1]:—

Izrail.—Here is one of the least servants of Mohamed, the King of the Faithful. Let some one be kind enough to come to the door, for I have a message to deliver.

Fatima (at the door).—Who is that knocking at the door? And what can have induced him so to do? Is his thunder-like voice going to strike my soul dead?

Izrail.—Know thou, O daughter of the Prophet, that I am a stranger come from a distant country to receive light from Mount Sinai of Arabia. Be pleased to open the door and allow me to enter, for I have a knot to be untied inside.

---

[1] The translation is taken from Sir L. Pelly's The Miracle Play of Hasan and Husein, p. 83.

The Prophet.—Dost thou not know, Fatima, who is he that knocks at the door?

Fatima.—No, father, I any unable to tell who that rough-spoken man is. I can only say that his dreadful voice has made me quite restless.

The Prophet.—It is he who continually grieves the heart of men; he who casts the dust of misery on the heads of poor widows. It is he, even the snatcher of the souls of men, Jinns, beasts, and birds; he can command a full view of the east and west at the same time.

Fatima.—Oh! what shall I do? The time of trouble has, after all, arrived, the hour of affliction approacheth. Come in, O thou Snatcher of Souls, and say what thou wishest to do, for thou art permitted by the Prophet to enter.

Izrail.—Peace be unto thee, O Mighty Sovereign! Peace be unto thee, O Sun of the World!

The Prophet.—On thee be both peace and honour! Thou art altogether welcome. What may thy object or message be? Tell us.

Izrail.—May I be offered unto thee, O thou King of Freedom and Liberty! The Creator of the World has sent me to the earth to thee, to know whether it be thy pleasure that I should transport thy soul from thy body to a garden of roses and jasmines, or whether thou preferest rather to live eternally on the earth. Thou mayest choose which thou likest best.

The Prophet.—In the pleasure-garden of this life every beautiful rose is attended with several piercing thorns, and the treasure of this world has many venomous serpents accompanying it. Thus thou mayest take my life if thou pleasest.

To return to the state of Mirza Hasan Khan, in despair a soothsayer was now called in. This individual, after repeating some cabalistic phrases, remarked that the patient had evidently been attacked by Jinns, either from passing along a canal at night without repeating the name of Allah, or else from putting his hand into hot ashes, which disturbs the young Jinns.

Neither of these things had Mirza Hasan Khan done; but still we felt that something might be effected by the soothsayer; and so, when he proposed to summon the king of the Jinns in order to inquire, we agreed.

Thereupon he asked for a basin of water; and we were all instructed to put money into it, in accordance with the love and regard we had for the patient. When I threw in a gold piece the soothsayer, with extraordinary gestures, chanted the following verse:

I adjure you, by the names of Allah, those of you who live in buildings and those who reside in deserts and uninhabited places, that you present yourselves before me to listen to my order and to execute it. All of you who are riding horses should appear, accompanied by your kings and princes; and all who are present or who are absent should appear, so that I may see you and speak to you in your own language, and obtain replies from you to the inquiries made from you as regards the treatment of this patient. Help, O Angels Rakyail, Jibrail,[1] Mekiail, Sarfiail, Ainail, Kamsail, in producing these Jinns.

Suddenly the soothsayer foamed at the mouth to make us believe that Shamhurash, the King of the Jinns, had entered him, and a dialogue ensued, during the course of which Mirza Hasan Khan was accused of various offences against the Jinns, such as sitting at night under a green tree without repeating the name of Allah; throwing stones at the heaps of house-sweepings, the usual place of rest at night of Jinns and their children; throwing a bone, and thereby hurting the Jinns; finishing his meals without leaving anything; or throwing a half-burnt piece of wood without uttering Allah's name.

At length it was decided that a black cock should be sacrificed, and a charm written with its blood and placed underneath the pillow of the patient, who also was ordered to eat its liver raw; but, alas! my dear uncle was dying, and, after mourners' tears had been administered in vain,[2] he was gently

---

[1] The Arabic form of Gabriel.
[2] Mourners' tears are collected during the "Passion Play" described in chapter xii., and are considered to be a sovereign remedy for all diseases. The clean handkerchief, in which the tears are gathered, is dried and placed in the shroud of the dead man.

laid with his face turned towards Mecca, while the "Yasin" chapter of the Koran was recited.

After this the dying man was called upon to make his will in the presence of witnesses; and he bequeathed one-third of his property for services in connection with his funeral, a pilgrimage by proxy to Mecca, and the reading of a special series of prayers at the shrine of the Imam Riza. The other two-thirds of his property, consisting of a house, a garden, and four parts of a village, were bequeathed to me. The document was first sealed by the dying man, then by Aga Mohamed and other witnesses.

MIRZA HASAN KHAN, MUSTAUFI

When the will was drawn up and thus completed, my uncle's seal was broken and placed at his right side; and his shroud was prepared, covered with the various prayers written by forty-one different individuals:

O Allah! we know certainly nothing but good about this person; but Thou knowest his condition better.

This is a testimony in favour of the deceased. And, as one of our deep-thinkers in utter humility and self-abasement wrote:—

We are ashamed to find on the Day of Judgment
That Thy forgiveness was too great to allow us to commit any sin.

When the death agony was passed my uncle's eyes were closed, and, after his limbs were stretched, the great toes of both feet were tied together and a scarf was bound round the head under the chin. The corpse was next placed on a bier, and after being carried round the court of the house, was taken to the Washing Place, preceded by Allah Mughari, termed the "Ministers of Death," whose duty it is, the moment a death has occurred, to ascend to the roof of the house and to chant in Persian:

Whosoever has come into this world is mortal;
The one who alone remains alive and everlasting is Allah.

Moreover, they chant the names and attributes of Allah in Arabic, whereby the fact of the decease is notified.

The corpse at the Washing Place was laid on a flat stone. The clothes were first removed, and it was washed with pure water, with water and soap, with water in which leaves of the lote tree had been mixed, and, finally, with camphor water. It was then wrapped in the shroud, which was fitted by tearing off suitable lengths, no thread or needle being allowed to touch it.

Two green willow sticks were placed under the arms, on which were traced, by the finger alone, the following words:

Certainly we know nothing but good of this person.

It is believed that so long as the sticks are left in the tomb, so long the corpse remains untouched by time.

When the corpse had been duly prepared, it was replaced on the bier and the funeral procession started for the cemetery. First came the relations, then the dead man carried by relays of voluntary bearers, and followed by a mullah on horseback, who recited the Al Rahman chapter of the Koran. Behind came numerous friends, and the procession was lengthened by led horses, sent as a mark of respect to the late Mustaufi; there was also a catafalque draped with black cloth, and numbers of people bearing unlighted candlesticks. In short, before the sad procession reached the cemetery at least a thousand people had joined it.

There the funeral prayer was recited by the mullah, and the bier was removed to the foot of the grave. Three times was it lifted from the ground and three times was it replaced. At the fourth time the corpse was gently lowered head-foremost into the grave.

Earth from the tomb of the Imam Husein at Kerbela was lightly thrown inside the shroud, the face of the corpse was uncovered and the right cheek laid on the bare ground, with a little of the sacred earth under it, the face itself being turned towards Mecca. The grave was first covered with bricks sufficiently high to allow the dead man to sit up and reply to the dread questions of Munkir and Nakir. Earth was then piled up and the mullah recited:

THE MULLAH

O Allah! this person is Thy slave, son of Thy man-slave and woman-slave. He is going to Thee and Thou art the best receiver of him.

Finally, water was sprinkled on the earth, and all present, opening their hands, buried their fingers in the soil in such a manner as to leave marks, reciting meanwhile the opening chapter of the Koran. As long as the finger-marks remain there the corpse will not, we believe, be subjected to any trouble. This concluded the burial ceremony.

But perhaps I ought to explain why these willow sticks are placed under the arms of the dead man, as otherwise the custom might appear to be without meaning, whereas the contrary is the case.

When the burial is completed and the mourners have dispersed, the mullah stays behind and, standing with his face turned towards Mecca, he solemnly adjures the dead man thrice in the following words: "Hear and understand! When the two angels visit thee and question thee, fear not; but reply by the confession of faith. Hast thou understood?" He then concludes, "May Allah keep thee firm in thy belief and guide thee!"

When the angels, Munkir and Nakir, visit the dead man, he raises himself into a sitting position on the two willow props. Standing one on each side, they straitly examine him, and, if the replies be satisfactory, they depart; but, if not, the corpse is beaten into dust by terrible fiery maces, and then again restored to its original shape.

If the deceased be a true Shia, whose replies have been found satisfactory, his spirit is taken to the "Abode of Peace" near Najaf to await the Day of Judgment; otherwise his soul is taken to the Sabra-i-Barahut, near Babylon, where it undergoes penance, and is purified against the same awful day.

The three following days were days of mourning. On the first day forty-one men were engaged to recite short prayers for the dead, to strengthen him in facing Munkir and Nakir; these are called the "Prayers of Alarm."

On the second day the grave was visited by relations and friends, and as the latter arrived they recited fatihas, or the opening chapter of the Koran, and ikhlas, or the last chapter but one of the Koran.

They then said, "May Allah give you patience and forgive the deceased, and may He make his position in heaven exalted!" After this they sat down with us and repeated fatihas and ikhlas, placing their hands on the grave.

Then we all stood in a circle, and the Reciter recited a prayer for the forgiveness of all the prophets and saints, and, last of all, for the forgiveness of the dead man.

We finally formed two rows, and thanked our numerous friends as they departed, saying, "Forgive the trouble," "You have taken infinite trouble." To this the reply was made, "May Allah show you his kindness, grant you patience, and reward you for your goodness!"

During the three days of mourning all our friends came to offer condolences. When they entered the house they sat down and softly recited a fatiha.

Sarsalamati, they then said, "May your life be safe!" Rose water was poured on the palms of their right hands, with which they sprinkled their faces; and, after drinking coffee, they picked up a portion of the Koran and read, or listened to the professional reciters, who recited chapters in a high-pitched tone. Finally, after partaking of tea and the water pipe, they withdrew to make room for fresh arrivals.

On the third day, the leading mujtahid, Aga Mohamed, came to bring the mourning to an end. He entered, observing the same ceremonial as the other visitors; and, after partaking of tea and a water pipe, he asked the relations of the dead man to fasten up the openings of their shirts which had been torn open as a sign of mourning, and to take off the shawl which the mourners, removing it from their waists, had wound round their necks. The Korans were then collected and a Sacred Recitation was held, at the termination of which all retired and the special part of the mourning came to an end.

Again, on the fourth morning, people assembled at our house, and listened to the Koran being recited. We were then taken to the cemetery, and after saying a, fatiha, I was escorted back to the Mustaufi's office, where I was welcomed, no longer as a mere assistant, but as the successor to the deceased Mirza Hasan Khan.

In order to show befitting respect for my late uncle, reciters remained for seven days reading the Koran over the grave. On the seventh day lamps and candles were placed on it; and had the deceased been prematurely cut off there would have been a larger number.

The ladies of the family lamented for the first three days with their friends, the same ceremonial being observed as in the assembly of the men; and, on the seventh day, they held a recitation on the grave and then retired. On Friday evenings, on the fortieth day, and again at the end of the year, similar ceremonies were performed. This was, of course, in addition to the festival of the Id-i-Barat. On this day, in honour of the birth of the twelfth Imam, all the souls of the dead receive a barat or bill of freedom for three days; and services are held, and food and sweetmeats distributed to the poor at the graves, which are adorned with flowers.

And thus, O my readers in Europe, respect us for the manner in which we reverence the dead, for whom we wear black clothes for forty days, during which period it is not permitted to use henna or to shave the head. Moreover, mourners do not attend any marriage ceremonies or parties of pleasure until the oldest member of the family takes them to the bath, where they have their hair cut and dyed and their beards trimmed.

Meanwhile a slab of stone had been ordered, bearing an inscription giving the name, family, and age of the late Mirza Hasan Khan, together with the date of his decease. Verses from the Koran and the names of the twelve Imams were also inscribed on it, and when we all visited the grave on the fortieth day, the slab was inspected and then erected over the grave.

Now I have finished this very sad chapter, and, as the poet writes:

Whosoever is born must depart from this world,
As annihilation must overtake every one.

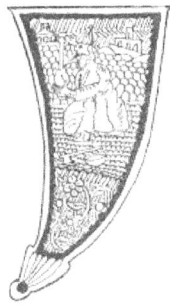

FROM A DAGGER SHEATH

MY FIRST MAMURIAT

FROM AN ENAMELLED BOX

A Mamur should be wise,
A ready talker, sharp witted,
And of independent disposition.
FIRDAUSI.

TOWARDS the end of the winter the Vakil-ul-Mulk, who had been Governor-General for some years, was summoned three or four times to the Telegraph Office, and there were rumours in the bazaar that he was to be dismissed. However, one day there came a private telegram from the Minister of the Interior, which ran as follows: "Alhamdu-lillah, after much trouble and discussion, your affair has been arranged. The Sovereign, may our souls be his sacrifice, condescends, in consideration of your capacity and efficiency, to order that you remain Governor-General of Kerman and Baluchistan."

The Vakil-ul-Mulk, who was much pleased, at once gave the Telegraph Master, who brought the auspicious message in person, five hundred tomans, and the following reply was despatched: "The kindness of the Sovereign has exalted the head of this lowly one, who ever prays that the shadow of His Majesty may eternally protect us. Ten thousand tomans, although not a fit present for the royal establishment, are offered by a bill on Aga Faraj Ullah."

Shortly after this it was decided to send a robe of honour of Kerman shawl to those governors who, by their efficiency and capacity, had been deemed fit to remain in office; for, praise be to Allah, the Vakil-ul-Mulk was not like one of his predecessors, who used to take a present from one man, appoint him to a governorship, and then almost immediately accept a present from a second man, and send him after the first with an order of dismissal.

About this former ruler there is a story which runs that he once appointed a man to a governorship, and this individual, knowing what to expect, bethought him of a plan by which he might be secured in his post. So one day, when the Governor-General was sitting at the window of the Hall of Audience, he saw such a one riding on a horse with his face to its tail and holding a paper in his hand. On seeing this, His Excellency remarked, "What animal is this?" and immediately ordered the individual to be brought to his presence and asked him what was the meaning of such behaviour. Such a one replied, "May I be your Sacrifice! This slave was appointed Governor of Bam; but, knowing that a second Governor would soon be appointed, he sat on his horse looking back towards Kerman and holding the order of appointment all ready for his successor!"

The Governor-General, upon hearing this, rolled over with inextinguishable laughter; and, when he was able to speak, he shouted, "Go, mount thy horse with thy head towards its head. I grant thee Bam for five years."

To resume, I was appointed Mamur to bear the robe of honour to Hidayat Khan, Governor of Jiruft. This official, who was thus honoured, had recently represented to the Governor-General that, owing to the lack of careful supervision, the Government land at Dosari had become worthless; but that he, to render a service to the State, was prepared to pay one thousand tomans for the property, although he knew that he would lose heavily by it. The Vakil-ul-Mulk, therefore, instructed me to also inquire into this question; and thus I felt that I was indeed a person of consequence when I started on my journey, with a well-equipped abdari on a stout pony, and three servants, one of whom, Rustam Beg, had served the deceased Mirza Hasan Khan as steward for many years.

But perhaps, O my readers in London, there are no abdaris in your country, and it is therefore necessary for me to explain their immense utility. The abdari consists of a pair of large leather saddle bags, faced with carpet, and in these are placed a samovar, a box of sundries, a set of round copper dishes with lids, in which food is carried, a tray, candlesticks, and many other things.

On the saddle bags the servant rides, sitting on a carpet or a Kerman felt of fawn colour, which, when needed, is spread for the meals or repose of the master. Behind is fastened a round leather case, in which all light articles, such as the water pipe, plates, spoons, etc., are carried. Add a charcoal brazier for lighting purposes, which swings on one side, a set of spits, and an umbrella, and you will agree that nothing more is needed than a mule laden with clothes and bedding for even such luxurious travellers as we Iranis, from whom you can learn something in the way of comfort.

Do not enter the tavern without the guide,
Although you may be the Alexander of your time.

The first town we reached was Mahun, where I stopped for a day to see my old friends, who all complimented me on my high position, and begged me to help them in their various cases. From Mahun we rode over a very lofty range, and spent the night close to its highest point in the caravanserai just completed by the noble Vakil-ul-Mulk. The building was of stone, and consisted of a splendid courtyard, round which were many small chambers, and behind were stables for five hundred horses or mules. In short, thanks to the generosity of the Vakil-ul-Mulk, we all passed an agreeable night, whereas, otherwise, it would have been too cold at this season of the year for sleep. Listen to what Omar Khayyam writes:

Think, in this batter'd Caravanserai
Whose Portals are alternate Night and Day,
 How Sultan after Sultan with his Pomp
Abode his destined Hour, and went his way.

We next halted at Rain, where a mullah insisted on entertaining me, although Rustam Beg warned me that the Aga was very avaricious. Indeed he spoke the truth, for, just as we were leaving on the following morning, his head servant came to tell me very confidentially that his master much admired my pistol.

I should have replied, "A gift"; but Rustam Beg interrupted me and said that the pistol was only lent me for the journey, and that it would not be right for me to part with it, even as a gift, to the Aga. He added that he himself was responsible for the return of the pistol to its owner. When the Aga's servant understood that he had failed he was very angry, so Rustam Beg said, "Bismillah! let us start quickly"; and when we had left the village behind he exclaimed, "By Allah! true is the proverb, 'None hath seen a snake's foot, an ant's eye, or a mullah's bread.' Praise be to Allah that I did not allow him to flay you!"

From Rain we travelled down a wide valley to Sarvistan, which is noted as being one of the windiest spots in Iran, the saying running as follows:

They asked the Wind "Where is thy home?" It replied, "My poor home is in Tahrud; but I occasionally visit Abarik and Sarvistan." [1]

Well do I recollect that it was necessary to order the luggage to be piled against the door that night, and, although this precaution prevented it flying open, it was impossible to sleep; and yet the villagers did not consider this gale more than a light breeze! May Allah take pity on them!

Separating us from Jiruft was the very high range of the Jabal Bariz, well termed "the Cold Range," as, although it wanted but twenty days to No Ruz, it was very difficult for our party to cross it owing to the deep snow.

We stopped for the night at Maskun; about a farsakh off is a famous cave, said to contain gas which kills all living things. Allah knows if this be true, but many witnesses agreed to its being so.

As a mamur from the Vakil-ul-Mulk, I was entertained by the head of the Jabalbarizis. He was evidently of a very great age—more than one hundred years, he said—and his face was like wax; but yet his eye resembled that of a hawk, and, in spite of his poor clothes, he bore himself like a king, and his long white beard was most majestic.

I asked him whether he had visited Kerman recently, as I found his features familiar; but he said that it was more than twenty years since he had left his district. That night, however, he narrated to me that he was a lineal descendant of Sultan Sanjar, from whom he was the thirty-fifth generation in descent; and suddenly I recollected that I had recently been reading a history of that great Seljuk monarch, who, once the Lord of half Asia, was defeated and taken prisoner by the vile tribe of the Ghazz. I also remembered that, in the history, was a portrait of the Sultan, and that that portrait resembled my host closely. The ways of Allah are concealed; but surely there is no other country in which its poor men can claim and prove that they are descended from Sultans.

---

[1] These places are close to one another.

IN THE JIRAL WARD

The world is nothing,
And the work of the world is nothing.

There was deep snow at Maskun; but yet, a few hours after leaving it, we descended into the valley of Jiruft, where it was already late spring, and it was delightful to see the green crops growing luxuriantly all round the groves of date palms. There were also large numbers of lambs and kids.

We were received by the confidential servant of the Governor, and entertained at a village situated on the right bank of the Halil Rud, the chief river of the Kerman province, which, from its violence, is also known as the Div Rud or "Demon River."

Close by stretched the ruins of the "City of Dakianus,"[1] covering many farsakhs. Now several ruined cities are termed by this name after a Sovereign, to escape whose persecutions seven Christian youths took refuge in a cave with a faithful dog, and there slept for three hundred and nine years, as recounted in the Koran. Two, farsakhs to the west is said to be the cave in which they slept; but I knew that this event took place in Asia Minor, and that this city was, in reality, the ruins of Komadin, which, so I have read, was the storehouse of the valuables of China and Cathay, and of Hindustan, Abyssinia, Zanzibar, and Egypt. By Allah, I felt sad when I thought of the fate of Komadin, sacked by the accursed Ghazz, who tortured its wretched inhabitants by pouring down their throats hot ashes known as "Ghazz coffee." May the curse of Allah be upon them!

Three days later, escorted by his staff and attendants, Hidayat Khan came out two, farsakhs from Dosari to a spot fixed by long custom for these important ceremonies. There I invested him with the robe of honour which had been, I assured him, worn by His Excellency the Governor-General, and was therefore, in truth, tanpush or "worn on the body," an especial honour. I also presented him with the order, by which he was reappointed Governor of Jiruft for the following year. Hidayat Khan was much pleased, and put on the robe of honour before the whole of the assembled Khans and people. He also placed the order on his head and eyes, and reverently kissed it before opening it.

To me he showed great kindness, not only on account of the deceased Mirza Hasan Khan, but also perhaps because I was now mustaufi in his place, and had charge of the revenue of the district. That night I was presented with a beautiful horse of Nejd race; and it was explained to me that an ordinary mamur would only have been given fifty tomans; but that I was to be considered an honoured friend and kinsman, as I was connected with Hidayat Khan through my mother.

Rustam Beg told me, with reference to the gift, that, before the just rule of the Vakil-ul-Mulk, a tyrant had been Governor-General of Kerman, who heard that Hidayat Khan possessed a Nejd mare of pure race. He tried to secure this by sending his Master of Horse to stay with the Khan, with orders to obtain it as a gift; but this plan the latter rendered worthless by

---

[1] Dakianus is the Roman Emperor Decius.

giving him butter which had been poisoned with copper, from which he nearly died. Indeed mamur's butter has become a proverb in the province.

Knowing, however, that the matter would have a sequel, the Khan sent off his family to Shiraz with the famous mare, and never slept in his house at night. By Allah! he was astute, as, a month later, fifty sowars suddenly surrounded his house at night, and, when they found neither the mare nor its master, they tied up and flogged all the servants, sacked the place, and then burned it. This Hidayat Khan saw from where he was living in a nomad tent a farsakh off; and he rode away to Shiraz, and thence went to Tehran, to prostrate himself at the foot of the Throne. But the tyrant was too powerful, and so he lived at Tehran for some years until that wicked Governor died, and he was free to return to Jiruft. My old servant concluded by telling me that the horse presented to me was of that same famous race.

The following morning I inspected the Government property, which, to judge from the quantity of weeds, was not well cultivated; but yet it appeared to be worth at least five thousand tomans; and I was informed that, if properly managed, it would yield crops worth two thousand tomans every year. For a day or two Rustam Beg was constantly visiting the Khan; and, finally, after much hard bargaining, and a threat to return to Kerman, it was arranged that I should receive two hundred tomans for my trouble, and that eight hundred tomans should be offered as a present to the Governor-General, if the Government agreed to the sale of the land at the price suggested.

In the meanwhile the Khan had paid me three hundred tomans which were due to the secretary of His Excellency for the cost of the robe of honour, the pay of the tailor, and the customary gift for the keeper of robes.

As it was very important to reach Kerman before the festival of No Ruz, because to travel during that period, according to our ideas, is inauspicious, I asked the Khan to allow me to leave and said good-bye to him.

Two of my horses having died from eating oleander, which is a terrible poison growing at the first stage, it was decided to snake a double march, and so Dosari was left in the middle of the night, and we rode through the pass with the oleander bushes without stopping, and finally halted at the hamlet of Saghdar. At this stage there was no snow left; but, on the contrary, even the camel thorn was beginning to show great buds.

Close to the hamlet was a party of gipsies; and Rustam Beg warned every one to be careful to see that they did not steal anything, when they came round playing their instruments and offering their pipe-stems for sale. These gipsies are the descendants of a band of twelve thousand Indian musicians and jugglers who were brought from India by Bahram Gur to amuse us Iranis; and, even to-day, they alone are the public musicians in most parts of Persia, although I have heard that, in Shiraz, Jews engage in this low profession. However, they are good ironworkers, and also they are experts at bleeding. Now we Iranis know that, unless we are cupped every spring and thereby purify our blood, we shall not retain good health during the summer; and thus their services are much in request for this purpose. In short, they are a vile race, but yet useful to us.

When we had recrossed the Jabal Bariz, we found that everywhere spring was coming; and we decided to march without any halts so as to reach Kerman some days before No Ruz. At Sarvistan, however, we met some men who had been robbed of everything except their trousers by a party of twenty-five Afshar bandits; and so, that night, it was decided to take an Istakhara, or beads, as to whether we should march the following day or wait for further news.

Now every Mussulman carries a rosary with one hundred beads, the origin of which is connected with the marriage of Her Highness the Princess Fatima.

The Prophet, on Him be Peace! declared that he would only give her in marriage to him on to whose house the planet Venus descended. That night all the suitors to her hand were watching the heavens from the roofs of their houses, when the planet moved from its place and descended to above Medina. The white Fatima, too, was watching; and, on seeing this marvel, she called out Allah ho Akbar, or "Allah is Great." When this exclamation had been repeated thirty-four times the planet began to circle round Medina, whereupon she exclaimed Subhan Ullah, or "Glory be to Allah." This she had repeated thirty-three times when the planet moved towards the house of Ali, and, finally, she broke into Alhamdulillah, or "Thanks be to Allah," which she repeated thirty-three times, while the planet stopped over the house of Ali, congratulated him on his good fortune, and re-ascended to its place in the firmament.

GIPSY MUSICIANS

These rosaries are consulted in case of danger, and indeed on every occasion. So the opening chapter of the Koran was first solemnly recited, after which I shut my eyes and, thinking intently about the dangers of the road, I took an unknown number of beads in my hand; and then counted them three at a time.

Every one was delighted when it was seen that there were ten beads, as one over, termed Subhan Ullah, is deemed to be most auspicious; and we immediately determined to proceed on the following day. Of course we kept our pistols and rifles all ready, but the route was deserted, although we saw where the Afshars had thrown away part of the loot which was useless to them; and, that night, we all felt very happy that we had been able to prove the truth of our proverb that "a road attacked by thieves is safe," which means that, after attacking a caravan, the robbers hasten away with their loot, knowing that they will be pursued.

In fact, that night a Captain with thirty sowars arrived, and, a week after our return to Kerman, they brought in seven of the thieves, who were publicly executed in the great square of Kerman, after which the executioner was given a present by all the shopkeepers, this being his perquisite.

During the last stage, the horses and mules understood that they were approaching their home, and moved quite a, farsakh an hour; and, in time, the walls of beloved Kerman appeared, and this my first mamuriat was successfully accomplished. Not only was the private secretary pleased with what I had brought him; but even His Excellency, after listening to the details of what I had done, condescended to praise my diligence and capacity, and remarked to the above official that such a one was a good servant.

FROM AN OLD BRASS TRAY

THE PERSIAN NEW YEAR

FROM A CARPET

> Yet Ah, that Spring should vanish with the Rose!
> That Youth's sweet-scented manuscript should close!
> The Nightingale that in the branches sang,
> Ah whence, and whither flown again, who knows!
> Omar Khayyam.

IT is one of the chief glories of Iran, that it has been ruled by monarchs who have become renowned throughout the Seven Climates. Perhaps the greatest among our many famous rulers was Jamshid, who introduced the use of iron, the art of weaving, the art of healing, and indeed many other arts, on which the happiness not only of Persia but of the entire world is based.

Among his inventions was that of wine, which was discovered in the following manner:—The King, who was immoderately fond of grapes, stored a quantity which fermented. Seeing this, he placed them in jars and had the word "poison" written on them. It happened that one of his wives, who was suffering from a torturing ailment, decided to commit suicide, and so drank of the contents of the jars, which immediately cured her. Jamshid and his courtiers thenceforward became addicted to the use of wine, which has, since that date, been known as "Sweet Poison."

By the orders of the Koran the drinking of wine is forbidden; but yet the habit has always been so strong among Persians that many of them still drink it, but always in private, and, generally, having the desire to give up the bad practice; also they repent when they yield to this weakness, and pray to Allah to grant them grace. By thus repenting, their prayers are perhaps accepted, for sincere repentance wins the favour of Heaven.

In truth, many Mussulmans would not approve of Hafiz when he writes:

Saki, come! my bowl rekindle with the light of lustrous wine; but they understand that the poet means by the Saki or Cupbearer the Spiritual Instructor, who hands a cup of celestial love, which is typified by wine.

However, in discussing this important question, Jamshid has been forgotten. He, apart from the wonderful discoveries made by him, was able, by means of his seven-ringed cup, not only to predict the future, but also to survey the entire world. In short, Jamshid ranks with Suliman or Solomon, son of David, as the lord of the Divs; and to-day there is the Takht-i-Suliman and also the Takht-i-Jamshid close together in Fars; and they say that there is no doubt whatever that the latter is much finer than the former.

I marvel when I read that, in Farangistan, the year begins in the "Forty days of Cold." Praise be to Allah, Jamshid decreed our New Year, both in accordance with nature and science.

With us the "Forty days of Cold" commence on the shortest day of the year, as is meet and befitting; and are succeeded by the "Small Forty Days," which are only, in reality, twenty days.

Major J. W. Watson, phot.

THE DERVISH AT NO RUZ

Now, seven days before the end of the great cold period we say that the earth breathes secretly, and that, twelve days later, it breathes openly.

When the "Small Forty Days" are ended there are two periods of ten days, known as Ahman and Bahman, as the old verse runs: This signifies that now there is no more fear of cold, albeit ten days before the festival is the "Season of the Old Woman," which, as its name implies, is sometimes very unpleasant and disagreeable.

Ahman has passed and Bahman has passed,
With whom should I please my heart?
I will take up a half-burnt piece of wood
And kindle flames throughout the world.

Meanwhile, however, the desert is becoming green and the blossom has begun to appear on the trees, and, as Omar Khayyam sings:

Irani indeed is gone with all his Rose,
And Jamshid's Sev'n-ring'd Cup where no one knows;
  But still a Ruby kindles in the Vine,
And many a Garden by the Water blows.

And David's lips are lockt; but in divine
High-piping Pehlevi, with "Wine! Wine! Wine!
  Red Wine!"—the Nightingale cries to the Rose
That sallow cheek of hers to incarnadine.
Come, fill the Cup, and in the fire of Spring
Your Winter-garment of Repentance fling:
  The Bird of Time has but a little way
To flutter—and the Bird is on the Wing.

At this period, just before the "Season of the Old Woman," dervishes pitch tents outside the houses of the great and recite prayers for their prosperity. It is customary to make them a handsome gift; but if this be not done quickly, they blow their horns at intervals during the night and, by rendering sleep impossible, loosen the purse-strings of the rich Khan or merchant. Indeed I have never forgotten the awe with which I regarded a dervish at Mahun, who possessed a beautifully inlaid axe of a great age, a begging bowl, on which the combat of Rustam with the White Div was carved, and a very fine lion's skin. While I was gazing in wonder at these articles, Ya Hu was pronounced like a lion's roar and my heart became like water. Ever since that date I have reverenced dervishes, as is but right and befitting.

I now come to the preparations for this our greatest festival. Some ten days before it, "House Shaking" is performed, every room being carefully swept and the carpets taken out and beaten. New clothes, too, are made for every member of the household. Already some wheat has been prepared by being wetted so that it sprouts by the great day. Special cakes of fine wheat-flour, with butter and sugar, are also baked; and the innumerable varieties of sweetmeats for which Yezd is especially famous: dried fruits and nuts are also provided.

On the last Wednesday before the fête, just before sunset, three fires of bushes are lighted in the courtyard, and every member of the household jumps over them, reciting "Paleness yours and redness ours," signifying thereby that all ill-health is left behind and ruddy cheeks will alone be seen in the future. Rue and mastich are mixed and held in the hands while jumping over the fires, and are thrown on them to avert misfortune.

At night pilao, in which slices of paste are mixed, is eaten; and an earthen-ware jar of water, in which some copper coins have been thrown, is hurled into the street from the housetop.

It is considered to be auspicious to keep all doors open; and it is the custom to take a good or bad omen from any conversation that may be overheard, the listeners standing on a key, the symbol of opening, and listening with bated breath.

If they hear such conversation as "Your place was empty. We spent a happy night," they creep away highly pleased; but, on the other hand, if they hear Allah forgive the deceased, he was a good companion," or "His disease has become so serious that neither medicine nor prayer has any effect," they feel that the New Year will be inauspicious.

Girls, too, who hope for marriage, are taken by a woman mullah to a place where four roads meet. There they sit with a lock fastened on to their dress and offer sweetmeats to passers-by. This is termed "Luck Opening," as every one who partakes of the sweetmeats first turns the key in the lock and thereby opens the way to good fortune for the damsel.

The night before the fête gifts of money are sewn up in small bags or wrapped in paper and presented on the fête day to each member of the family, and the poor are not forgotten. The bath is then visited and, after careful dyeing of the hair, the new clothes are donned. On this occasion every one cuts his nails and throws the parings into running water, thereby losing all bad luck.

Upon returning home, two hours before the equinox, a white cloth is spread with seven articles, all of which commence with the letter "S," such as sirka or vinegar, sib or apple, etc. etc. All fruits, and more especially melons, which have been carefully preserved throughout the winter, are also set on the table, with sweetmeats and dried fruits.

Eggs dyed red are also baked and eaten by all, the mother eating one for each of her offspring. Candles, to the number of the children in the house, are lighted, and, above all, a live fish is placed in a bowl which, when the new year begins, instinctively turns towards Mecca.

Milk is kept boiling as a sign of abundance, a prayer carpet is spread, and the following prayer is repeated three hundred and sixty-six times:

O the Turner of the hearts and eyes!
O the Lord of night and day!
O the Changer of conditions and dispositions,
Turn Thou our condition and better it.

Gold coins and wheat are now held in the palm of the hand, as also the woodlouse, an insect which brings good luck; and as the New Year commences, the sweetmeats and fruit are distributed, and every one gazes at the woodlouse for choice; or, if not, at a narcissus, at water, or at red clothes.

The gate of the house is shut an hour before the equinox, and no one is allowed to enter from outside; but, as soon as the new year commences, the master of the house goes out into the street with some sweetmeats, and after having distributed them and walked about, he re-enters his house.

Visiting and feasting are then the order of the day; and every woman who enters a house from outside must do so with her veil half-lifted, so that her eyes and eyebrows are visible; only women who have come to wash a dead body enter closely veiled.

People known to be unlucky, or those who bring ill luck to others, such as executioners or members of their families, are rigidly excluded on this day. In this connection there is the story told of Shah Abbas who, when starting on a hunting expedition which proved to be a failure, first looked at an ugly old man.

Upon his return he sent for him, intending to kill him. The man asked why he should be doomed to die; and the Shah said, "Because thy ill-omened visage has spoilt my hunting." The intended victim retorted, "May I be thy Sacrifice! but thy visage will be still more ill-omened if it brings death with it." Upon hearing this, Shah Abbas laughed and dismissed the man with a gift.

For twelve days no work is done, nor can any enterprise or journey be undertaken. On the thirteenth day the house is unswept, and every one goes outside and sits in the green wheat. If the house be not left absolutely empty, misfortune will take up its abode there.

Before the day has set, it is most auspicious for ladies to pound up three peas' weight of pearls with sugar and swallow the mixture; and every one who can afford it performs this rite. Alhamdulillah! pearls are abundant in Persia, as they are found mainly in the Sea of Fars.

I think that, in this brief account of No Ruz, I have explained how every one, whether rich or poor, rejoices that the winter has passed, and that the time of flowers, of the glory of the gardens, and of the sweet song of the bulbul is approaching. As the poet Kaani wrote most beautifully:

It is the New Year's Day. O Saki, hand the cup round;
Do not heed the turn of the wheel and the revolution of the heavens.
O Turk, the sin [1] of the cup is enough for me on the New Year's day:
I do not care for the seven sin, as the dregs of wine suffice for me.
The people are talking of new clothes;

---

[1] Sin is the letter "S" as previously explained.

But I am longing for a cup of wine filled to the brim.
Every one places sweetmeats on his tablecloth and utters prayers;
But I wish for abuse from thy sweet ruby lips.
Every one holds silver and grains of wheat in his hands;
But I prefer the grain of the mole on thy silvery face.
Pistachios and almonds are the relish of the festival for others:
But, with thy lips and eyes, I do not want pistachios and almonds.
Men burn Ud [1] on New Year's day, and I am lamenting like an Ud
For one who, with her black mole, will spoil Islam.
People kiss each other and I am dying of grief;
Why should another kiss that sweet-lipped one?
Vinegar is placed on the tablecloth by every one;
And my beloved wrinkles her rosy face into vinegar with anger.

At this season, too, it is customary to play games; and, in every open space, both men and boys play leap-frog, rounders, tip-cat, and other games, while, outside the city, the sons of our Khans throw the javelin at full gallop, and then catch it as it rebounds from the ground.

They also practise galloping past an egg placed on a little mound of earth; and so perfect is the marksmanship of our best sowars that, with a single shot, they break this egg; and it always makes me proud to think that the hearts of our enemies would be bigger than eggs, and that none of them could escape from the unerring bullets of the sowars of the victorious Shah.

Now we also practise marksmanship on foot; and one of the high officials of His Excellency used to throw up copper coins into the air, which were almost always hit by our Governor-General with his rifle. This official used to ask us courtiers to give two kran pieces for His Excellency to shoot at; but we only saw copper coins used, and when we remonstrated, this astute individual always replied that it was his perquisite, and after all, he underwent much trouble in this business, as if the Governor-General were unsuccessful he always abused the official for throwing up the coins in a stupid fashion; also, once or twice, the bullet passed just over his head; and so there was danger in what he did.

But, in my opinion, nothing that is done in the way of exercises at No Ruz is so important as the science of wrestling, in which we Kermanis surpass all

---

[1] Ud is aloes wood; and the word also means a musical instrument.

Persians, just as Persians excel all other nations. Now I propose to give you some details about wrestling.

The patron saint of pahlawans or wrestlers is Puriavali, who was a famous champion. He was, on one occasion, travelling to the capital to wrestle with the chief wrestler of the Shah, when, near the City Gate, he saw an old woman distributing sweetmeats. Inquiring the reason of this charity, the old woman replied that she was doing this to invoke the aid of the Imams to give her son, who was to wrestle with Puriavali on the morrow, victory over the latter, as she depended on him for her daily bread.

On hearing this, Puriavali was so moved that he made a vow that he would constrain himself to be beaten by the son. Indeed, his inward eyes were opened, and he, at that instant, miraculously attained sanctity.

On the morrow, when he closed with his rival, he allowed himself to be thrown on his back in the first bout, to the great surprise of the spectators and to the intense indignation of his forty followers. When the contest was over, he informed the latter that they should leave him and go their ways, as his soul had attained a state of rest which he could not obtain by mere brute force; and, from that day until he died, he led the life of a saint.

The "House of Force" is a room with sitting places all round lighted by skylights. In the middle a six-sided pit is dug about seven feet deep. Dry bushes are brought and packed closely together, with their roots in the ground. A mat is spread over them, and soft earth or horse litter is heaped on to a height of a foot and a half. The surface is then trampled upon until it becomes soft and smooth.

To the west of the pit the Murshid's raised dais is set next to the entrance to the arena, which is purposely built so that persons entering it should be obliged to bend very low as a sign of humility.

The Murshid sits on the dais and a bell attached to a chain hangs over his head. A feather is fastened to the bell in memory of any champion who learned his profession and attained fame in the school, just as Nadir Shah wore four feathers in his crown to show that he was monarch of Persia, India, Afghanistan, and Bokhara. A drum and a samovar are also placed on the dais.

The Murshid is generally a dervish, who has devoted himself to the theoretical and spiritual side of wrestling, although sometimes he is a retired champion. He plays on the drum and recites verses while the pahlawans are exercising or wrestling, and at the end of the performance he distributes hot water and sugar.

When a wrestler is about to enter the arena he kisses the threshold and salutes the Murshid, "Peace be on thee, O Murshid." The latter replies "Peace be on thee, O pahlawan, Thou bringest blessing." The Murshid also swings the bell when the chief wrestler enters the arena. The pahlawan kisses the edge of the Murshid's dais and passes into the arena. He then puts on the wrestler's drawers, which he first kisses. They are made of stout cloth, and descend to below the knees, with leather knee-caps and a leather thong round the waist.

The first exercise generally consists in passing the arms through two slabs of stone, each weighing about 90 lbs.; and, lying on the back, each slab is alternately raised by rolling the body to one side and then to the other. This is to strengthen the shoulders.

Another exercise consists in "swimming" on a board, during which the Murshid recites the poem beginning with:
The Emperor of China had a daughter like a moon;
But who has seen a moon with two raven tresses?

After that clubs are brought in and the Murshid recites: To conclude these preliminary exercises, each pahlawan in turns whirls round the pit.

The rose trees are in bud and the nightingales are intoxicated;
The world has attained its majority; and lovers sit down to a feast.

I hope that by the above description I have explained how very perfect and complete are the exercises for wrestling in Persia; and I now ask you to accompany me to, see the match which had been the theme of conversation in Kerman since the autumn, for it then became known that the chief wrestler of the Shah, Isfandiar Beg, who was a Kermani, had, upon visiting his home, been challenged by the chief of the Kerman pahlawans, Abdulla Beg, who had never been defeated.

Three days before the match took place, a notice was posted up that there would be "Strewing of Roses"; and, in honour of the announcement, all the coffee houses and shops in the vicinity were gaily decorated, as indeed was the wrestling school, the pillars of which were draped with valuable Kerman shawls. Flowers, too, were profusely displayed; but, on the Murshid's dais, there was only the battle-axe, the horn and the begging bowl of the dervish, arranged on a lion's skin. Two peacocks' feathers, one in honour of each champion, were suspended over the bell.

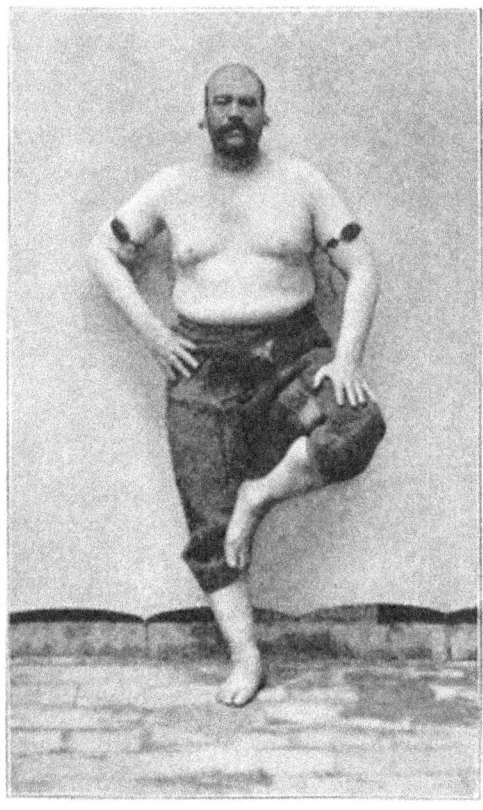

THE SHAH'S WRESTLER

On the day of the match the "House of Force" was filled from early dawn; but it was not until two hours before sunset that His Excellency the Governor-General arrived and the Murshid asked permission to begin the contest. This being granted the two wrestlers were introduced; and, by Allah, perhaps they were the two strongest men in the world.

The Shah's wrestler, who was several years the older, appeared to be like a massive tower, in fact if anything too heavy. He had, however, the reputation of being very alert and quick of eye, and full of tricks. Indeed he was known by the sobriquet of "Tricky."

Abdulla Beg, on the other hand, was as perfect as a picture and well proportioned. His head round and of medium size, his ears small, his eyes big, his nose straight, his face dry and fleshless, his neck long and thick, his chest broad and deep, showing his capacity to hold his breath. His arms were long, and, in the upper part, were three muscles termed "little fish"; his forearms full, his wrists hard and fleshless, his fingers drawn and straight, his waist small, his thighs full, the calves of his legs muscular and showing great development, and his feet arched. Indeed, he was so perfect a man that every one burst into acclamations of surprise and praise.

The respected head of the quarter, who was a Sayyid, and himself an old wrestler, first addressed the champions, and warned them not to bear malice against one another; he then joined their hands and the wrestling began, after the permission of the Murshid had been received, and the latter then recited: Then he broke into reciting the "Flower of Wrestling," beginning,

Puriavali said that the quarry is in my lasso,
And that by the help of David my fortune is high.
If however thou thirstest for grace, learn humility,
Because land which is high can never receive water. [1]

In valour and bravery thou art the bravest in the world:
In the presence of thy cypress-like body, the cypress itself has no worth.

The moment the hands of these two pahlawans had touched one another, they sprang in opposite directions, each taking up a position. Abdulla Beg, full of pride, would stand erect whilst his opponent was bending his body and was looking exactly like a fighting cock. Then they began to move round and round, always on the look-out to secure an advantage over the

---

[1] This refers to land cultivated by means of irrigation.

other. Now they closed and again they separated. Then they put one hand on the back of the neck of the other.

The Shah's pahlawan at this point being more alert than Abdulla Beg, bent down and, dodging his head under Abdulla Beg's left arm, was, in the twinkling of an eye, behind his back; but the latter finally shook him off. Both men received applause for the skill and strength shown in this bout.

Again they closed and again they separated. The fourth time, Abdulla Beg got behind his opponent, and seizing the leather belt, tried to roll him on his back. The Shah's wrestler, in turning suddenly, thrust his fingers into the eyes of Abdulla Beg, whereupon the latter throwing him on the ground, pressed with his chest on Isfandiar Beg's back and head so furiously that, in two or three places, his adversary's skin was rubbed off. The Shah's wrestler then bit Abdulla Beg's hand; and the latter bit the other's ears.

Blood began to flow and the spectators became excited, and the Governor-General, seeing that it was not fair play, ordered his head farrash to separate the combatants. They would, however, not separate; so other farrashes were called in, and, by dint of beating both the men, they separated them.

The spectators were now thoroughly excited, some taking the side of the one and some of the other; and a wealthy young merchant from Tehran, who was backing Isfandiar Beg for a large sum, became so furious that he drew his revolver. The Governor-General abused him and told his men to take it away, which was done.

After some words of advice from the Governor-General and the old Sayyid, the two pahlawans took up exactly the same position as at first, and a really fine display of wrestling now commenced. It was evident to every one that Abdulla Beg was gradually getting the better of his opponent, who had lost his wind. He was, in fact, turning him by sheer force on to his back, and the onlookers believed that he had won when a miracle happened; and, before we could collect our senses, we saw Abdulla Beg lying flat on his back.

It happened in this way. When Abdulla Beg was attempting to overturn his adversary, the Shah's pahlawan got hold of one of his legs with his locked hands and began to turn round and round, when, all of a sudden, pulling the leg inwards and throwing his weight against Abdulla Beg, he overturned him. This was one of those tricks which wrestlers are encouraged to practise in the great cities.

The spectators now got up and all was confusion, some crying that the pahlawans must wrestle again, others shouting that the match was over, until the Governor-General threatened to take strong measures, when comparative calm was restored.

His Excellency then summoned the two pahlawans to his presence, and remarked that both had done very well; he presented a shawl to each man, and, as Abdulla Beg's arms had not been tattooed, he ordered that a lion should be tattooed on his right arm in memory of this great contest.

The spectators, too, gave gifts of money, and the merchant from Tehran made peace between the two champions and invited them both to a feast, where he compared the Shah's wrestler to Rustam, and Abdulla Beg to Sohrab, and pleased them both by quoting:

Two Forces, two Arms, and two bold heroes;
One a dragon and the other a lion.
Two fierce tigers or two colossal elephants;
Or two skilful wrestlers.
They began to wrestle,
Holding each other by the waist.
They pressed each other so hard
That breathing became difficult for them.
Several blows were exchanged with such vindictiveness:
That the earth quaked beneath their feet.
Each again caught hold of the other,
The one like a lion and the other like a leopard; Both tried their best,
But neither would own defeat.
Each one attempted to overpower the other,
And the desert became muddy with blood.
The wrestling of these two heroes was such
That the names of Rustam and Sohrab were forgotten.

DETAIL FROM A KERMAN CARPET

THE PILGRIMAGE IS VOWED

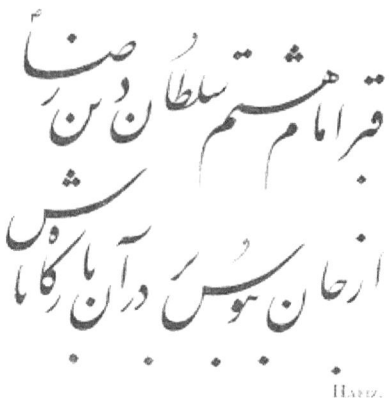

From thy soul, kiss the grave of the
Eighth Imam, Riza, the Sultan
Of the Religion; and remain
At the Gate of that Court.
Hafiz.

MANY years had elapsed since the events narrated in the last two chapters. Among other things, the second Vakil-ul-Mulk, may Allah forgive him! had died, and a Governor-General, who was a stranger to Kerman, had been appointed.

During the previous winter a comet, which always portends calamity, had appeared. There had been very little snow or rain, and in the spring the scanty crops were eaten up by locusts. The result was that wheat which, the year before, had been sold for four tomans a kharwar, now fetched eighteen tomans. In short, famine had fallen on the province.

Had the Vakil-ul-Mulk been alive, he would have sent a thousand camels to Sistan at his own expense to bring wheat to the city; but the new Governor-General only cut off the ears of the bakers when they sold their bread, made chiefly from millet, dear, and finally baked the chief baker alive in his own oven.

Allah knows that bakers in Persia are scamps, but this action produced no good result, as all the merchants who would have sent money to buy wheat from the other provinces were afraid that it would be seized by the mamurs, whom the Governor-General placed on every road, and who made matters worse, as they beat the camel-drivers and stopped the caravans until they received money; and so even dates and rice were not sent to Kerman, which was like a city besieged by enemies.

At last, however, His Excellency removed the mamurs, and then rice and dates reached the bazaar; but during that summer people mainly lived on fruit, which is a most unwholesome diet.

To add to our calamities cholera broke out in the province. In the spring travellers had brought it from Baghdad to Tehran, whence it had reached holy Meshed. However, owing to the healthiness of Kerman and its distance from Meshed, it seemed probable that it would escape this calamity; but Allah, the Omnipotent, no doubt wished to punish us for our sins; and a returning pilgrim died of cholera at a village only one stage from Kerman.

This, too, need not have infected our beloved city, but his clothes were brought in and washed in a stream which passes through the gardens inhabited by the Gabrs.

It happened that there was a wedding that night at the house of Arbab Shahriar, the chief of the tribe; and before morning, the bridegroom, the bride, and seventeen of the guests were infected, all of whom died.

There is no place for pleasure between the Earth and the Heaven;
How can a grain escape from between two mill-stones?

When this calamity was known in the city, it became a Day of Judgment; and everybody fled who could. Now, although we Iranis are noted for our bravery in battle, I must confess that all of us, owing to our highly-strung nerves, which are the result of living in a very dry climate, fear the cholera, as if an attack of it were tantamount to the Angel of Death knocking at the door.

Even our noble Governor-General fled to a valley, where he posted his troops down below, to prevent any one from passing them; and he himself, with one servant, camped above near a tiny spring, and threatened to shoot any one who, on any pretence whatever, approached him.

The Vizier, too, was equally afraid; and, as he had heard that cholera never attacked people underground, he took refuge in a disused well and remained there for forty days. Since the Doctor Sahib, who laughed at us for being afraid without reason, and attended the sick throughout, informed me that by boiling all water and only eating cooked food, all cause of fear would be removed, I remained at Kerman with my family. Another reason for this was that my garden in the Bagh-i-Zirisf was watered by its own water channel.

However, many of my servants, acting against the Prophet's tradition, which runs, "At the outbreak of an epidemic abide where ye are, as fleeing from a place is to escape from death to death," fled to their homes and, later, I heard that all had died on the road, whereas, praise be to Allah, no one in my family, or indeed in the Bagh-i-Zirisf, was attacked.

After a month the cholera ceased in Kerman, but was raging in the adjoining villages; so the Governor-General, who had been sternly ordered by the Shah to return to his post, and had been informed that he was considered to be the shepherd of the people, now gave orders that no one should enter Kerman without undergoing quarantine.

This, by Allah! was very astute, as the winter was setting in, and all the mullahs, Khans, and merchants gladly paid large sums of money to be allowed to return to their homes.

The English laughed at them; but, in truth, it is not that the English are braver than we Iranis. Allah forbid! I have read that their country is so wet and so foggy that their ideas come very slowly in consequence; and so they do not realise dangers as quickly as we Iranis. I represented this to the Doctor Sahib, who laughed immoderately, and said, "By Allah, that is the reason the French give for our defeating Napoleon!"

Now I had vowed a solemn vow that if the Imam, on Him be Peace! protected me and my family during this awful calamity, I would hasten to prostrate myself at his threshold. Consequently, when every one had returned and had congratulated me on my phenomenal courage, I explained the matter to them, and more especially to Mahmud Khan, who had occasionally stated that he too wished to participate in this grace.

Now I have not hitherto mentioned Mahmud Khan, who was among the great people of Kerman, and who was a relation of my family. When a youth he had entered the college which Nasir-u-Din Shah, may Allah keep cool his Grave! had, at that time, recently opened in order to teach the young princes and Khans all European learning.

Mahmud Khan, however, so they say, was very stupid, and, after six months, the professors represented to the Shah that they had beaten him daily, imprisoned him, and indeed tried to teach him by every possible means, but in vain; and they had all sealed a declaration to the effect that he was incapable of receiving instruction.

The Shah, upon hearing this, reflected for a while and then said, "As thou art proved to be incapable of receiving instruction, it is better that thou returnest to thy home. Perhaps there thou wilt learn to distinguish between wheat and barley. Thou art dismissed."

This happened many years ago; and as Mahmud Khan inherited twenty villages in the districts of Bardsir and Rafsinjan, and spent his whole time in looking after them, he became very rich.

Another thing aided this, namely, that he was miserly and would not have thrown a bone to the dog of the Seven Sleepers. Thanks be to Allah, we Iranis are, as a rule, very liberal, and we fully agree with Shaykh Sadi who wrote:

Generosity will be the harvest of life.
Freshen the heart of the world by generosity;
For ever be steadfast in generosity;
Since the Creator of the soul is beneficent.

But Mahmud Khan was so miserly that his horses were always hungry, so much so that one of them once attacked a man dressed in a green coat, thinking it was fodder! Also he kept the key of the storeroom himself, and every day gave out a very little butter and a very little rice for the daily food of himself and servants. Indeed, had he not been very stupid, no servant would have remained in his service.

MAHMUD KHAN

Yet he was most fond of Europeans, and was the first Khan to be friendly to the Doctor Sahib. Indeed, he promised to give him land on which to build a hospital, and for three days he rode to his numerous gardens with the Sahib, and asked him to decide which one he considered to possess the most suitable air for the purpose.

However, he finally settled that he could not give any of his land, and so the matter remained, although occasionally His Excellency the Governor-General used to say in jest, "Well, Mahmud Khan, when is the hospital going to be built?" And he replied, "I beg to represent that I am busy with the matter."

One day His Excellency informed the Khan that he wished to be his guest in his garden, and, although Mahmud Khan knew exactly what was right to do in such cases, he was too avaricious to incur the necessary expenditure. His Excellency was not pleased, and when in the afternoon he called together all the Khans, he turned the conversation on to the subject of avarice and miserliness, by saying that he had recently heard of a merchant of Isfahan, who was so mean that he ate his bread dry, and only took enough butter to cover the tip of a needle with the last mouthful. He added that he doubted whether any one could be more miserly than that.

Shaykh Ahmad, however, represented that he knew of a man who, every day, took a handkerchief to the grocer and bought a little flour, which he afterwards returned, complaining that it was mouldy. At the same time some flour stuck to the handkerchief, which he was careful not to shake; and, by doing this at several shops, he collected enough flour for a loaf of bread, and this he cooked himself with bits of bushes which dropped off the donkey-loads as they passed through the bazaars. For relish, he went about and sat down where he could smell the cooking of the kabobs in the coffee-houses. His Excellency agreed that Shaykh Ahmad had given even a better example than his own. Abu Turab Khan then represented that he had heard of a still worse case of a rich merchant of Yezd, who only allowed each member of his family a piece of dry bread to eat. One day his daughter, who was very beautiful, but whom no one would marry on account of the father's evil reputation, took compassion on a poor old beggar and gave him her piece of bread.

Her mother, in the kindness of her heart, recommended that the girl should be given another piece, but the father, hearing what had happened, became like a madman, and not only cut off his daughter's right hand, but turned her out of the house into the streets of the town.

The poor girl wandered about, not knowing where to go, when she was seen by the Governor-General, who was returning from a hunting expedition. Moved by her beauty and innocence, he took her to his women's apartments and, seeing the nobility of her disposition, finally married her to his son.

On the wedding night the bride placed a bowl of sherbet before her husband with her left hand, and he, feeling shocked at this lack of good manners, quitted the room to complain to his mother. Meanwhile the girl prostrated herself on the ground, crying out, "O Allah! why dost Thou suffer a creature to be humiliated for want of a hand which performed a good deed for Thy sake? Either restore my hand or strike me dead."

The bridegroom, who had now for the first time heard from his mother of the noble act of the girl, returned, when the bowl of sherbet was again set before him by the bride, and this time with her right hand, which Allah the Omnipotent had restored. The youth was amazed, and prostrated himself to thank Allah for giving him as a wife a maiden who had received such a signal favour from heaven.

The next day the miserly merchant was summoned, and, as he could offer no excuse for his barbarous conduct, he was sentenced to have both his hands cut off and to be killed by having food rammed down his throat. His daughter, however, interceded for him and he was pardoned, and it is stated that he repented, and, proceeding on a pilgrimage, died on the way.

After this His Excellency said nothing, and when he rose up to leave, it was evident that he was displeased with his host to whom he showed no kindness. The result was bad for Mahmud Khan, as, after His Excellency had finished his repast, his servants broke all the dishes, including four china sherbet bowls which had been in the Khan's family for many generations. As Naushirwan the Just truly said:

The slave who is bought and sold is freer than the miser:
For the slave may one day be free, but the miser never.

Mahmud Khan was of a very powerful build and wore long moustaches, which, when he twisted them, made him look very fierce; and indeed he was noted for his bravery, as, on one occasion, he rode alone after a band of seven Afshar robbers and killed three of them.

Another story, too, he used to tell, which was that, one evening, he was in the mountains and just finishing his prayers, when a leopard attacked him, but with one blow from his sword he cut off its head, which he nailed up over his gate, just as lovers of sport fasten the skulls and horns of wild sheep.

The Khan informed me that he had decided to take Ali Khan, his son-in-law, with him. Now this youth, unlike his father-in-law, was very small and slight, so that he was sometimes compared to a sparrow. He was one of the Khans of Bam, and his ancestor rendered a great service to the Kajar dynasty by seizing Lutf Ali Khan, Zand. This proud warrior held Kerman for many months against the might of Aga Mohamed Shah, whose entrenchments are still standing; but, seeing that there was no hope except in flight, he escaped from the city and fled to Bam, where he was seized and thrown into chains.

Ali Khan, on this account, and also because he owned much property in Narmashir, where the best henna in the world grows, was very proud and quick-tempered, but yet the Khans of Kerman, if not as rich as those of Bam, always consider themselves nobler and higher, and it was deemed a great honour for Ali Khan to become the son-in-law of Mahmud Khan.

When this important question had been decided, we had many meetings and discussions as to what date we should start on, and what route would be the best to follow. We soon agreed that a few days after the festival of No Ruz would be a suitable date, but it was very difficult to fix on the route.

The direct track lies across the Great Desert for half the distance, and Mahmud Khan said that he wished to travel that way because he hoped one day to construct a road by which pilgrims could drive to the Sacred City. At this, Ali Khan, who was, in truth, a light youth, laughed behind Mahmud Khan's back, and whispered that he was not likely to have leisure from building the hospital to devote to constructing a road.

We finally persuaded Mahmud Khan to travel by Yezd, as to that important city the road is good, and the desert is only fifty farsakhs wide at this point. Moreover, I represented to him that by travelling this way he would be able to visit his villages in Rafsinjan; but what made him finally agree was that I said forage and food were much cheaper by the Yezd route, and that in Rafsinjan he would obtain everything free of cost.

Thus he agreed, and for the next four months we were busy making all the necessary arrangements, buying mules and horses, and also the necessary outfit. The most difficult point was to settle which servants to take and which to leave behind, as they represented that it would be an act of merit on my part to arrange for them all to go.

However, that too was ultimately arranged by Rustam Beg stating that he had already been twice to Meshed, and that he would not feel happy if any one but himself was left in charge of the house and property, but that he did not require any other personal servant to stay behind with him.

It remains to refer to the religious exercises to which we delivered ourselves before starting on this solemn pilgrimage. Each of us, in turn, held a meeting at which the calamities experienced by Ali, Husein, and the other holy Imams were recited.

The black-hearted people who slew the offspring of the Prophet with malice;
They claim to belong to the religion but murder the Lord of the Religion;
They commit to memory the Koran and draw the sword, reciting the chapter Taha;
They wear the Yasin chapter as an amulet; but murder the acknowledged Imam.

Afterwards, we entertained our relatives and friends at luncheon and received gifts for the road, such as tea cups, tea, and other such useful presents.

In short, owing to the arrangements which had to be made and these meetings, the winter passed very quickly, after which there was very little leisure left before the actual day of starting.

DETAIL FROM A KERMAN CARPET

YEZD, THE PRISON OF ALEXANDER

FROM A NOMAD CARPET

> I was afraid of the Prison of Alexander;
> And fled to the Country of Solomon. [1]
> Hafiz.

AGAIN the joyous festival of No Ruz came round, and when its thirteen days were passed it was high time to beat the drum of departure. At last the Chief Astrologer pronounced a certain Thursday to be a propitious date, and that evening, accompanied by hundreds of relatives and friends, we started for a garden which is situated about a farsakh from beautiful Kerman. It may be thought that this was a very short stage for travellers who had such a long journey before them; but the fact is that we Persians have more experience of travelling than any other nation, and so we understand that on such occasions much is invariably left behind. In truth, upon reaching the garden every servant found that he had forgotten something; and, but for this custom of ours, termed "Change of Place," our position would have been difficult.

I have not mentioned that, as soon as it was known that some of the leading inhabitants of Kerman were about to undertake the pilgrimage, at least fifty of our fellow-citizens decided to accompany us; and as it is a pious deed to facilitate pilgrimages, we agreed to allow them our protection on the road.

The following day we marched a full stage, and the third day brought us to Kakh, the chief village of the district of Khinaman; it is a very ancient

---

[1] Sc. Fars.

village, so much so that I have read that it supplied to the armies of the Sasanian monarchs seven intrepid warriors mounted on bulls. Its Governor besought us to halt a day; but Mahmud Khan refused, and, on the fourth day after starting on this journey of grace, we entered the district of Rafsinjan, which is renowned for its pistachio nuts and almonds. Indeed, so delicate are the shells of the latter that they are known as "paper."

Mahmud Khan insisted on our halting for two days while he visited his villages, and, as the Governor of Rafsinjan was a well-known Khan of Kerman, it was very agreeable to stay there in his service, and to give him the latest news of His Excellency the Governor-General and of Kerman.

Husein Ali Khan had ruled Rafsinjan for over twenty years, in fact ever since he had rendered a signal service to the Shah by killing a rebel Buchakchi chief. This wild bandit for a long time refused to visit the Khan and make his submission; but, at last, the latter sent him a Koran sealed with his seal, and the promise that, so long as he was on the earth, no harm should happen to him. The Buchakchi, upon seeing the Koran and hearing the promise, finally came into Rafsinjan; but the Khan, who was very astute, sat in a specially prepared pit underground, and, being thus freed from his oath, shot the bandit who had killed hundreds of travellers. To reward him for this great service the title of "Amir of Amirs" was bestowed upon the Khan, who, a few years later, again showed immense capacity in the art of government.

It happened that one of the Hindus, of whom there are several at Kerman, was robbed and murdered in the Rafsinjan district; and the English Consul Sahib sent repeated telegrams to the English Legation, with the result that every day fresh orders came from the Minister of the Interior for the murderers of this Hindu to be caught and punished; there was also a threat of dismissal unless this was done quickly.

Now all the while the Governor knew who the robbers were, but he did not wish to show great severity, as, after all, the killing of a Hindu was not a great crime. However, he was obliged. to seize the men and informed the Consul Sahib of the fact, and that he was ready to have them executed. But that official, who had been hard throughout, to his surprise refused to have the men executed without proofs of their guilt.

The "Amir of Amirs" pondered for a while, and then asked the interpreter of the Consulate to go into an adjoining room and expect the proof desired by the Sahib. The prisoners were now brought in, and all the, farrashes were dismissed.

The Khan then spoke most affectionately to them and said, "O my brethren, we are all Mussulmans, and I, like you, rejoice at the death of this infidel, may his soul remain in Hell! I have dismissed all my servants that I might secretly congratulate you; and I wish to know to whom the most credit in this meritorious deed is due." Hearing this, Iskandar Khan replied: "Praise be to the Allah, we were all partners in this pious deed. Ibrahim Khan seized the Hindu, Abdulla Khan held his donkey, and I shot the infidel, and Allah knows he bled like a pig."

No sooner had he finished than the Governor called out "Bacha!" [1] and, when his farrashes returned, he asked the interpreter if he was at last satisfied of the guilt of the prisoners, and, upon his replying in the affirmative, he ordered the executioner to take them to the Great Square and execute them. That dread official afterwards mentioned that the men were as if in a dream, and never seemed to realise what was happening, so simple were they that they could not understand the astuteness of a high Persian official.

Upon leaving Rafsinjan we rode to visit the famous "Well of the World." It is a mighty chasm in the desert, and a great river flows beneath it. They say that every year many camels, sheep, and goats tumble into it and are carried away, so great is its force. One day this water, if Allah wishes, will be used for cultivating the waste land of Rafsinjan, and indeed it resembles an untouched gold mine.

The next place of importance on our journey was Anar, which contains a shrine dedicated to Mohamed Salih bin Musa Kazim. In it is a Koran stand, made of sandal wood, in which ivory is inlaid, and it is so beautifully carved that the work of to-day is nothing in comparison.

The Governor at the time was Murtaza Kuli Khan, Afshar, who was appointed to this, a frontier district of the province, as the Lashanis and other Fars tribes all feared him because of his cruelty. It is related that

---

[1] Lit. "Boy." Servants in Persia are invariably summoned in this manner.

once, when riding near Anar, he saw a child tumble into a mill-race. One of his servants galloped forward to save it, but he shouted out, "Stop and let us see what will happen." Thus, by his lack of humanity, he deprived a poor widow of her only son whom she relied on to provide bread for her old age, when he grew up.

The day before our arrival he had committed a still more terrible deed. One of the leading landowners had some months before complained of his tyrannical behaviour, and the Governor-General had rebuked him for oppressing the people he ruled. Upon receiving this message from Kerman, he had summoned the landowner and addressed him as follows: "Thou art the first man who has been brave enough to complain of me to the Governor-General, and thy heart must be different from other men's hearts." He then roared out to the Chief Executioner, "Take out his heart and let me see it." The bloody order was instantly carried out, yet even this did not sate his fury for vengeance, for he also refused to allow the corpse to be buried.

THE KORAN STAND AT ANAR
(Dated A.D. 1359)

As a result of this terrible outrage the whole population of Anar had taken sanctuary at the Telegraph Office, the wires of which terminate at the "Foot of the Throne."

At first the telegraphchi, who received fifty tomans every month as a gift from the Governor, refused to send their petitions either to Tehran or to Kerman, so the villagers threatened him and his family with instant death. Upon this he complied, and he explained afterwards that he really intended to help them all the time, as he was horrified at the crime; but he feared that, unless he could plead that his life was threatened, the savage Governor might kill him too.

Glory be to Allah! no sooner was the state of affairs explained than most severe orders came for Murtaza Kuli Khan to proceed by post to Kerman, where he met with the punishment he deserved. By Allah! I think that he was really mad.

Three stages of desert with salt water had now to be traversed, and Mahmud Khan narrated to us that this desert was haunted by vampires, who attack men overcome by sleep, and drain their life-blood by licking the soles of their feet. He added that, some years ago, two muleteers whom he knew lost their way in a storm in this very desert, and finally, being utterly tired out, were obliged to go to sleep until the morning. They were much afraid of the vampire; but, being clever Kermanis, they decided to lie down feet to feet and so fell asleep. Shortly afterwards the dreaded vampire came upon them, and began to prowl round them to discover their feet; but at each end it found a head.

In despair it fled, exclaiming: With such stories did we pass the time on these three stages, in which the water is so salt that to drink it causes nausea; but yet it is impossible for the sons of Adam to exist without water, and so we consoled ourselves by feeling that the greater our privations the greater the merit of our pilgrimage; and I quoted:

I have wandered through one thousand
Six hundred and sixty-six valleys,
But nowhere have I seen a two-headed man.

Consider hardship as ease if the matter be important. Upon hearing this every one became happy, and the desert stages were quickly passed.

Throughout the journey Ali Khan was always trying to shoot partridges; but he was not a good shot; and when, at last, he brought one into the stage, and with much pride presented it to Mahmud Khan, the latter exclaimed, "Of course it was sick."

At last we reached the province of Yezd, and that night we halted but a short stage from one of the famous cities of Iran.

Yezd was the first city of our mighty empire other than Kerman which I had visited, and, by Allah, well does it merit its reputation of having served as a prison house in which Iskandar imprisoned his enemies, the refractory Divs. Indeed, when approaching it, I was assured that the city was quite close; this, however, I could not believe, as all I saw was a hideous desert of sandhills, a fit abode for Ghouls and Afrits, but nothing else.

Even as this thought came into my mind a dreadful wind began to blow, and everything was black as night. However, we rode on like brave Persians and dimly saw two high towers, which, had I not been possessed of much wisdom, I should infallibly have mistaken for a castle built by the Divs. At last some mean mud garden walls appeared, and riding between them, we had entered Yezd.

YEZD AND ITS WIND TOWERS

Yezd is indeed an unfortunate town, as, after having served as a prison to Iskandar, it was founded as a city by Yezdigird, whose evil title was "the Sinner." Indeed so wicked was he that Allah the Omnipotent did not permit him to die an ordinary death; but, when he visited the sacred lake of Su, in the mountains of Nishapur, a white horse suddenly appeared out of the lake, kicked the monarch so that he died, and then as suddenly disappeared in the waters of the lake.

To come down to later times, too, my father, may Allah forgive him! I well remember used to mention how that when Fath Ali Shah was the Sign of the power of Allah, and Yezd had the honour of being ruled by Mohamed Ali Mirza, one of his sons, a certain Abdur Razzak Khan, not only rebelled, but insulted and outraged the Prince's family. However, Abbas Mirza, the Rustam of his age, seized the criminal, who was handed over to Mohamed Ali Mirza. He, a true drinker of blood, with one stroke of his victorious sword smote off the accursed rebel's head.

The Yezdis are so cowardly that nowadays no soldiers are drawn from the population, and, indeed, what can be expected of a people which lives in a country of sandhills, where even the milk cannot be drunk, as it both tastes and smells so strongly of cotton seed, on which alone the cows are kept alive? It was a regiment of Yezdis who, after returning from the conquest of India, asked the great Nadir to give them an escort to see them to their home. But yet, although entirely lacking in manliness, the Yezdis are good weavers, and some of the silk they manufacture is esteemed highly in Persia, although, of course, it is not as famous as the shawls of Kerman.

Sad to say it was a Yezdi who introduced smoking opium among us, and, alas for Iran! why has this calamity befallen us? Allah knows but I would blow from a gun those who introduced this accursed habit.

First of all, the opium is smoked with charcoal; then the miserable man ever craves for something stronger, until he smokes opium once burnt, and thereby concentrated, in an old, much used pipe which is heated over a lamp.

The Doctor Sahib told me that whenever a mullah attacked him for holding the religion of Hazrat Isa, on Him be Peace! he invariably replied that rather than that there should be divisions among the "Possessors of a revealed book," it was better for the entire strength of both religions to be exerted to stop this calamity. And by Allah this is true, as Hafiz says:

If grief should array its army to shed the lover's blood,
I and the Saki will unite to destroy grief.

The ruler of Yezd was one of the princes of the Royal family who, when I was honoured by appearing in his presence, showed me particular notice, and said, "Thou art well known to me, Nurullah Khan, by thy poems. Inshallah! while thou remainest at Yezd thou art my guest."

In truth, not only was I treated with great distinction, but before we left the Master of Horse of His Highness brought me a beautiful Arab horse with its tail dyed scarlet, thereby showing that it came from the royal stables. In return, I wrote a panegyric on the horse and His Highness, who, I afterwards heard, said that his name would, on this account, never be forgotten in Iran. It ran as follows:

Bravo the Charger with hoofs like Shabdiz [1] and a head like Rakhsh, [2]
Awaji [3] on the dam's side, whose sire was Yahmum. [4]
Sometimes he is like a bird in gliding and a snake in twisting;
Sometimes he dances like a pheasant and bounds like a ball.
An alligator in the sea and a leopard on the mountain.
A crane in the air and a peacock in the street.
He gallops without urging or inciting.
Fiery as the angel of fire: and in water like a duck.
His muscles are tight like a bow-string, his sinews like armour, and his mouth well-shaped,
His head a date palm, his tail a cord, his flanks of stone and his hoofs sharp-edged.
A late sleeper but an early riser, fleet and far-seeing:
Easy to handle, a good goer: well-behaved and well-bred,
Hard-footed, tough-thighed, straight-legged and round-hoofed.

---

[1] Shabdiz was the famous charger of Khusru Parviz and Rakhsh, the equally famous charger of Rustam, as mentioned in Chapter II.
[2] Shabdiz was the famous charger of Khusru Parviz and Rakhsh, the equally famous charger of Rustam, as mentioned in Chapter II.
[3] Awaji and Yahmum are a mare and horse respectively, renowned in Arab poetry.
[4] Awaji and Yahmum are a mare and horse respectively, renowned in Arab poetry.

Sharp-eared, flat-backed, smooth-skinned and short-haired.
Fleet as the clouds, swift as the wind: in thunder like lightning and also in his stride.
Destroyer of mountains, Splitter of storms, Scaler of cliffs and Discoverer of roads.
With legs of a wild ass, liver of a lion, pace of a leopard and the determination of a racer:
Throat of an elephant, breast of a rhinoceros: the jump of an ibex and the disposition of a wolf.
Sharp-eyed, iron-livered, steel-hearted and hard-lipped:
With teeth of silver, nostril like a well, throat like a tube, and a brow like a tablet.
Spear, sword, lasso, battle-axe, arrow and bow
Are his neck, ear, tail, hoof, mouth and leg.
The Governor has given me such a horse without a saddle,
Such a horse is like a jar without a handle.

That night the Master of Horse again came with a message from His Highness to the effect that he had originally given orders for one of his own saddles with gold trappings to be sent with the horse, and that he hoped the negligence of his servants would be forgiven. He asked me to inspect the holsters, in which I found a pair of gold-mounted pistols, and, overwhelmed at the munificence of the noble Kajar prince, I exclaimed, "By Allah! Hatim Tai has returned to life."

ROBBED IN THE LUT

FROM AN ENAMELLED BOX

> Therefore we delivered Lot and his family,
> Except his wife; she was one of those
> Who stayed behind: and we rained
> A shower of stones upon them . . . and
> We turned those cities upside down.
> The Koran.

WE had reached Yezd on the sixth day of the sacred month of Muharram; and this we had purposely intended, as, being pilgrims, we were especially bound to take part in this sad anniversary. In a previous chapter I referred very briefly to the difference between us Shias and the Sunnis. I will now give further details, as, indeed, I then promised.

We know that when, for the last time, Mohamed, on Him and on his family be Peace! performed the pilgrimage, known as the Farewell Pilgrimage, the angel Gabriel came to him at Mecca, with instructions from Allah, the All-Wise, to proclaim publicly that Ali should be his successor.

Upon the conclusion of the pilgrimage the Prophet, accompanied by Ali and his other companions, started on his return journey, and, at a village termed Khumm, close by which there was a pool of water, the solemn investiture was held. A throne, constructed of camel saddles, was erected, and Ali was set thereon by the Prophet, who then embraced the "Lion of Allah" in such a close and long embrace that, by this act, his virtues were transmitted to his illustrious son-in-law. Finally, the Prophet formally constituted Ali as his successor and heir; and this historical event is annually celebrated with much rejoicing under the name of "the Festival of the Pool of Khumm," wherever Persians reside.

However, owing to the wickedness of mankind, Abu Bekr, Omar and Osman were all elected Caliphs before Ali came to his right, and he only ruled for a few short years, being foully murdered in the sixth year of his Caliphate. After his death, his eldest son, Hasan the Pious, succeeded him; but being wearied with the faithlessness of the Arabs, he abdicated, and, like his descendant the Imam Riza, was poisoned.

Ten years later his brother Husein, who had been promised the succession to the Caliphate upon the death of Muavia, was invited by the fickle Kufans to trust himself to their support to win the throne which was justly his, and, accompanied by a small band of his faithful followers and his family, he started off on this ill-omened journey.

Upon his approach the Kufans, the curse of Allah be on them! deserted the cause of the Imam, who declined to retire but resolved to die fighting to the bitter end, being fortified in this resolution by the vision of a phantom horseman who said to him, "Men travel by night, and by night their destinies travel towards them."

He encamped with his small party at a place called Kerbela, near the bank of the Euphrates, and, to ensure a desperate defence, ordered the tents to be fastened together, to prevent an attack from that quarter.

In the morning both sides prepared for battle, the forces of the enemy being under Umar bin Saad, who was bribed to oppose the Imam by the promise of the governorship of Rei. He himself wrote the following verse on the subject:—

Shall I govern Rei, the object of my desire?
Shall I be accursed for slaying Husein?
The murder of Husein damns me to inevitable flames:
Yet sweet is the Possession of Rei.

Umar's force numbered four thousand, whereas the band of the Imam consisted of but seventy-two devoted followers. However, before the battle commenced, Al Hurr, an Arab chief, who commanded thirty horsemen, quitted the ranks of the enemy and joined the sacred force with his son, brother and slave, the other sowars declining to follow him. By Allah! we reverence his memory even to-day and remember how he reproached the Arabs in these words: "Alas for you! you invited him and he came, and you not only deceived him, but are now come out to fight against him. Nay, you have hindered him and his wives and his family from the waters of the Euphrates, where Jews and Christians and Sabæans drink, and where pigs and dogs disport themselves."

When the battle commenced two warriors stepped forth from the ranks of the enemy, but they and many other champions were slain by the indomitable heroes, until Umar withdrew his horsemen and sent five hundred archers to the front, who rained in arrows. Even then the warriors of the Imam were unconquered until, after the fight had raged the whole day, and the entire party of the Imam had been slain, the Imam himself, overpowered by countless wounds, fell in a last desperate rush among the foemen. May the Peace of Allah be on him, and His forgiveness be on the members of his band and on Al Hurr!

LEADERS OF THE MUHARRAM PROCESSION

The helpless women were stripped and insulted by their captors and also by the pitiless rabble on the way to Damascus, where the accursed Yezid, son of Muavia, endeavoured to aggravate their sorrows in such a fashion that it can never be forgotten.

It is this awful tragedy that we Shias celebrate in the month of Muharram, and on the tenth day, the anniversary of the murder of the Imam Husein, the Prince of Martyrs, there are always processions to remind us of the heart-rending calamity. In Yezd each of the seventeen quarters prepares a procession, the cost of which is partly defrayed by the legacies of pious men.

The procession I joined was headed by a band of men who, to honour the Imam by self-inflicted pain, had hung horse-shoes, locks, and heavy chains to their bare bodies, and who, by their example, encouraged even little children to wound themselves in memory of the wounds of the Imam.

Then came camels laden with tents, and innumerable mules, lent by their pious owners, carrying baggage, followed by a hundred horses with shawls draped on their necks and by two hundred led horses. Behind these there were thirty-five camels, ridden by members of the Imam's family, representations of the seventy-two bodies of the martyrs, seventeen heads on lances and a band of Arab horsemen. Two singers of war songs represented the two parties and engaged in a heated dialogue, mingled with curses.

Then came Hazrat Abbas, the standard-bearer, accompanied by eighty water-carriers. It was he who was slain when attempting to draw water from the Euphrates.

Among the most conspicuous features was a wooden house draped in black to represent the bridal chamber of Fatima, daughter of the Imam, who was married to her cousin Kasim just before the fatal day. A hundred dervishes with their axes, horns, and lion or leopard skins also formed part of the procession.

The next scene was that of Yezid on his throne, surrounded by his Court, while eighty men beat two stones together and recited mournful verses. Nor must we forget the ambassador from Europe, who, seeing Yezid insult the head of the dead Imam, fearlessly rebuked him before all his courtiers. Finally, there was a model of the tomb of the Imam, surrounded by brave officers and soldiers of the ever-victorious army of Iran.

In the different parts of the procession groups of two hundred men beat their breasts in rhythm, and as they advanced they recited:

THE MUHARRAM AT YEZD
(Showing the Bier of the Imam in the background)

O our Imam Jafar! [1]
Husein our Lord
Has been murdered on the plain of Kerbela;
Dust be on our heads.

And so the procession moved in stately order to the square of Mir Chakmak, where there is an octagonal, tile-covered pillar, which is peculiar to Yezd. There a halt was made, while an enormous structure, representing the bier of the Imam, decorated with fine Kerman shawls and innumerable flags, mirrors, swords, and daggers, was slowly carried round the Square by five hundred men, who bore this heavy burden as a sacred privilege. It is the pride of the inhabitants of the village of Mohamedabad to render this unique service to the Imam; and nowhere else in Persia is there such a huge bier. From the Square the procession proceeded to the Palace, where the Governor loaded its organisers with gifts and released two prisoners convicted of murder; and so back to its quarter, after having shown to men,

---

[1] Jafar was the sixth Imam.

women, and children the poignant tragedy of Kerbela, which will not be forgotten by us Iranis until the Day of Judgment.

After taking part in the procession on the tenth of Moharram, we decided to continue our journey across the dreadful Lut to Tabas without undue delay. As I am deeply versed in geography, and am not among those who believe that "Atlantic" is the name of a city, perhaps the people of London would like to hear from me about our famous desert, for, just as the gardens of Iran surpass all others for beauty, so the Lut, well named after one of our prophets, Lut or Lot, on Him be Peace! surpasses all other deserts in the world for its extent and aridity.

Now the Lut stretches from near Tehran across the centre of Persia to the frontiers of Baluchistan, a distance of two hundred farsakhs, and, if travellers speak the truth, this desert really stretches almost to India; but only in Iran is it called the Lut. From north to south its extent is nowhere more than one hundred farsakhs wide, and, by the road we were travelling, it scarcely exceeds fifty farsakhs in width.

This huge desert was once, according to our histories, a sea; but nowadays there are great ranges without water and vast areas of moving sand, which covers the road if there be a strong wind. Again, there are huge salt swamps, more especially in the northern portion, and elsewhere it is so stony that it is necessary to travel very slowly. Throughout there is very little water, and generally it is salt. Indeed, there are countless steep passes over the ever-barring ranges of hills, fearful ascents and descents, dangerous swamps, and the terror of the moving sands. The climate is either extremely hot or bitterly cold. Indeed only a brave and hardy race like we Iranis would dare to cross such an awesome place, which is not only haunted by Ghouls and Afrits, but also by robbers with savage faces and evil hearts.

There is no water, no habitation, and
No summons to prayers of the Mussulman.

In all this huge waterless tract there is unlimited grazing for camels, but little else. I have read that the camel-bird [1] in ancient days inhabited this

---

[1] This is the Persian term for the ostrich, which ranged the Lut many hundreds of years ago.

desert, and the Doctor Sahib told me that the English in Africa now make much profit from selling its feathers. In the name of Allah, then, let them come and show us Persians how to become rich from our boundless Lut!

We resumed our journey on a propitious day; but, just as I was mounting, Ali Khan sneezed violently, and had not Mahmud Khan, who declined to pay an extra day's hire for the mules, prevented us, we should not have started that day. Allah knows how true is our proverb, "Greediness makes a man blind."

About a farsakh from Yezd we dismounted to smoke a water pipe, and, sitting on a ridge overlooking the city, we swore with an oath that it was not fit for any one to live in but the Yezdis. As Ali Khan truly remarked, the city was composed mainly of wind-towers. [1]

We rode slowly forward, and as we were descending a little valley, a hare suddenly crossed our track to the left. Mahmud Khan turned white like curds at this evil omen; but, angry at his behaviour in the morning, I pointed out that what fate ordained would be; and that avarice was composed of three letters, and that all three were empty. [2]

In truth, I could not content myself with this proverb, but said to them, "Have you not heard the story about the late Commander-in-Chief of the Persian army at Tabriz?" This personage was so avaricious that he used to allow the regiments on duty to return to their homes only if their officers paid him large sums of money.

This was his constant habit, until he was very ill and the Angel of Death was knocking at the gate, when he was told that General Najaf Ali Khan had come to see him about dismissing the Muzaffari regiment; but that, as he was ill, he would not be allowed to trouble him.

Unable to speak, the dying man gave a sign that the petitioner should be admitted; and the General, after a few words, offered one thousand tomans. The Commander-in-Chief was in the death agony; but, just before

---

[1] These wind-towers are high chimneys, and convey a draught of air to subterraneous rooms which are resorted to during the summer.
[2] This refers to the Persian word for avarice, which is spelt by three letters, none of which are dotted.

the Angel of Death seized his soul, he shook two lean fingers at the General, signifying thereby that he must pay two thousand tomans, and, shaking his two fingers, he died. Truly Allah is great and his paths are hidden!

To complete my ill-humour, when we halted to eat our breakfast my servant Gholam Riza represented to me that my samovar had evidently been stolen at Yezd, as he could not find it in the morning when packing up. He added that this was fate. This answer made me so angry that I exclaimed, "Thou half-boiled jackass, dost thou not know what our Prophet, on him and on his family be Peace, replied to such a one as thou?" He ordered: "Tie up the knee of thy camel, with thy trust in Allah." Better advice than this has no man given.

The following day the head muleteer suggested to us to ride about a farsakh to the left of the track, as we should see the famous City of Lut. And indeed it was a wonderful spectacle, as, on each side of a wide valley we saw the ruins of great forts and of wonderful buildings, so enormous and so magnificent that they must have been built by the Divs. Here then was the country which Allah the Omnipotent destroyed, as it is written in the Koran, "We turned those cities upside down." O my brethren, tremble and fear the vengeance of Allah the Omnipotent! and forget not the awful punishment that fell on those evil-doers.

That night at Kharana we overtook a caravan of pilgrims from Shiraz, who had been delayed for a week by rumours that a band of robbers was holding the road. However, the arrival of our party, sixty strong, doubled our numbers; and it was decided to march together until Meshed was reached.

In the caravan from Shiraz were two Khans with whom we made acquaintance. But it must be stated clearly that, in the whole of Persia, there are no people so immoderately proud of themselves as the Shirazis. Indeed, before we had been together an hour, the son of Assad Ullah Khan quoted from Shaykh Sadi: Fortunately, I was as well acquainted with the great poet's works as the Khan, and I stopped this boasting for a while by quoting:

Judge with thine eyes and set thy foot in the garden fair and free,
And tread the jessamine under foot, and the flowers of the Judas tree.

O joyous and gay is the New Year's Day, and in Shiraz most of all,
Even the stranger forgets his home and becomes its willing thrall.

My soul is weary of Shiraz, utterly sick and sad;
If you seek for news of my doings, you will have to ask at Baghdad.

However, it was no use as, whatever we said, our companions could not realise that it was their good fortune at having two such poets as Shaykh Sadi and Khoja Hafiz born at Shiraz that had made their city known, whereas actually its climate is damp and unwholesome compared with Kerman, and in size there is no comparison. To say more would be excessive.

The morning we left Kharana it was arranged that we Khans with our armed servants should ride in front of the caravan in order to protect it; and we warned all the pilgrims not to straggle. No one would, however, pay attention to our warning, and the Chaoush,[1] who was reading suitable passages from the Koran, to which every one replied by Salawat or "Blessings," said that we should not be troubled, as His Highness the Imam Riza would protect his servants.

We stopped for the heat of the day at Rizab, a dilapidated, sinister-looking caravanserai. We knew that this was a dangerous place, as we had been informed that robbers from Fars had been heard of quite recently in the vicinity; but, to our delight, we found the place empty, and, feeling much relieved, we ate our breakfast with relish.

Mahmud Khan ordered two of his servants, as a precaution, to keep watch, and we all composed ourselves to sleep about noon. Just as we thought it was time to arouse ourselves and finish the stage, a terrible uproar occurred, and, before we had time even to seize our rifles, we were captured by the Fars robbers.

Their leader, Gholam Ali, was a man of most ferocious aspect, and when he recognised Assad Ullah Khan, he glared at him like a Div. Assad Ullah Khan was frozen to the spot like a statue; and it was explained that he had some years ago cut off the fingers of the right hand of Gholam Ali, who was

---

[1] The Chaoush is the leader of the party. He generally carries a flag on a lance and protests that he is the bravest of the brave.

caught robbing a caravan near Dehbid, of which village Assad Ullah Khan was at that time the Governor. The blackhearted ruffian, whose nickname was "Cut Hand," was so furious that his eyes became red, and he swore that, in revenge: he would shoe Assad Ullah Khan with horse-shoes; [1] and that he would only grant him a respite until he had collected the booty.

H. R. Sykes, phot.

THE CARAVANSERAI AT RIZAB

Everything belonging to us was seized. Personally I had not brought much money with me, as I had a bill on a banker at Meshed, and had sent the horse presented to me by the prince back to Kerman; but Mahmud Khan, who was old fashioned and loved to keep his money under his quilt at night, had seven hundred tomans with him, and in spite of his curses and entreaties all of it was taken. As the verse runs:

---

[1] This has frequently been done, death generally resulting.

GHOLAM ALI, "CUT HAND"
(Only the thumb of the right hand is left)

A MESHED BANKER

You may shout or cry; but the thief will not return the robbed goods. Our carpets, clothes, and rifles were seized; but the property of a mullah, who was a Sayyid, was restored. In short, we were stripped of everything except our underclothes, and those who resisted were badly beaten.

O readers of London and the New World, imagine our sad plight as we, who in the morning had owned horses, mules, and camp equipment, crawled miserably into Saghand with but a lame mule and a donkey which the robbers did not require. Ali Khan alone, like the light youth he was, kept repeating: "Respect is in Contentment; Disgrace is in Avarice," until we all begged him for Allah's sake to hold his peace.

Mahmud Khan was violently angry and behaved like a madman, at one time cursing the robbers, and at another vowing that his two servants, who had been ordered to keep watch, but who had slept, should eat a thousand sticks.

Everything, fortunately, has an end; but, upon our arrival at Saghand in a pitiful state of fatigue, judge of our surprise when we saw Assad Ullah Khan seated outside the house of the headman of the village smoking a water pipe. "O Allah, what do I behold? Am I asleep or awake?" and a thousand other expressions rose to our lips; but the Khan said, "Did you not know that the Shirazis are clever, and I who am not less clever than the other Shirazis, told the servant of Gholam Ali, who was guarding me, that I had two hundred tomans sewn up in my quilt. He, like all ass, believing me went off to find the money; and I quietly stole behind the caravanserai where Gholam Ali had left his horses, mounted one of them and, riding down a water-course, escaped. He completed his story by quoting: "If Allah wills, an enemy becomes a source of good."

At Saghand we met Haji Aga Mohamed, a merchant of Kerman, and, thanks to him, we were able to continue our journey without having to beg for our bread. Indeed, like the masters of wisdom that we were, we gradually ceased to eat grief, and Mahmud Khan finally forgave his servants, who incessantly begged me with tears to intercede for them, which I was bound to do. In short, I represented to Mahmud Khan that "Allah takes the boat whither He will; let the boatman tear his clothes in grief."

THE ARRIVAL AT THE SACRED THRESHOLD

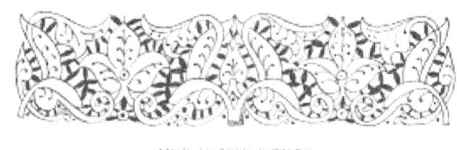

FROM LUSTRED POTTERY

> When Yunus fled into the laden ship; and
> Those who were on board cast lots among
> Themselves, and he was condemned; and the
> Fish swallowed him. . . . And We cast him
> On the naked shore, and he was sick; and We
> Caused a plant of a gourd to grow up over him.
> The Koran.

HALF-WAY across the Lut was a land of moving sands known as the "Sand of the Camels"; and here we endured much trouble, as we had only been able to hire donkeys at Saghand, and owing to the heat and the absence of water, we all suffered terribly. Indeed several of the pilgrims, most of whom were half-naked and on foot, fell down and remained senseless until the evening; but, praise be to Allah, they finally reached the stage where, although the water was salt, they all drank to repletion, so much so that the caravan had to halt for two days, as every one was ill, owing to the heat, thirst, fatigue, and, above all, the salt water. Yet we were very thankful that there had not been a storm, as many a caravan has lost its way and all its members have perished when the wind has moved the sands and covered up the track.

We were now in Khorasan, the Land of the Sun, and as it is one of the great provinces of Iran, it is advisable for me to briefly describe it. Khorasan stretches from the extreme north-east of Persia down to the province of Sistan, which is included in the same government, and which was the home of Rustam, the mighty champion of Iran.

Among the famous cities of the province are Tus, built by one of the generals of Kei Khusru and Nishapur, founded by the Sasanian monarch Shapur. To-day, however, owing to the Shrine of the Imam Riza, Peace be on Him, Meshed is the capital of this vast province.

I have read in the Shah Nama that it was at Kishmar, in the district of Turshiz, that Zoroaster planted a cypress, brought by him from Paradise, to commemorate the conversion to the new faith of Gushtasp, the Shah. For many centuries this cypress increased in size, until, fourteen hundred and fifty years after it was planted, the Caliph Mutawakkil ordered it to be felled and to be transported to Samara on the Tigris, where he was building a new palace.

The hapless Gabrs offered large sums of money in vain, and the tree was cut down, but the night before it reached its destination the Caliph was murdered by his son. I mention this story to show how very ancient and glorious a province Khorasan is, as it is now more than a thousand years since the death of Mutawakkil.

Khorasan, indeed, has many wonderful places. Among them is the fort of Kalat-i-Nadiri, which was undoubtedly built by the Divs, as it consists of a valley surrounded by hills which only a bird can cross, so precipitous are they.

In it Nadir Shah collected all the jewels and gold which he brought back from India, where his victorious army reduced its monarch to be his servant. This fortress, which is only defended at the five closed entrances, is one of the marvels of the world, and not even Amir Timur could capture it, as none of his soldiers could fly; and we Iranis may sleep in security so long as Bam in the south and Kalat-i-Nadiri in the north are garrisoned by the ever-wakeful troops of the mighty Shah, whose honour and glory are increased by the possession of these two great fortresses, which are famous throughout the Seven Climates.

As to the people of Khorasan I cannot entirely praise them, indeed they are noted throughout Iran for being dull and stupid; but then every one agrees that it is the Kermanis and Shirazis who are the cleverest and wittiest people in Persia, whereas in the north there are too many Turks, who are slow and dull.

To prove this stupidity of the Khorasanis, there is the story of three Persians who were each praising their own provinces. The Kermani said, "Kerman produces fruit of seven colours"; the Shirazi continued, "The water of Ruknabad issues from the rock"; but the poor Khorasani could only say, "From Khorasan come fools like myself."

However, I think that the Khorasanis, if dull, are very honest and very hospitable; and during my stay in their province I always found them most polite, and, as the poet says:

Whomsoever thou seest in the saintly garb,
Suppose him to be a good man and a Saint.

After traversing the terrible Lut, where we had suffered not only from the difficulties and dangers of the road, but also from the savageness of man, Tabas, the gate of Khorasan, as it is well named, appeared to us as beautiful as Damascus did to the Prophet. May the Peace of Allah be on Him and on His family!

In truth, when we rode up an avenue bordered on both sides by mulberries, elms, willows, and palms, and saw the streams of running water, we thanked Allah the Bountiful that we had, at last, arrived safely in an inhabited country after all our sufferings.

Tabas is termed Tabas of the Date Palm, to distinguish it from Tabas of the Jujube Tree in the district of Kain. It has always been famous not only for its dates and oranges, but also for its heat. Indeed, in Khorasan, to say "Go to Tabas" is not a polite remark.

Many centuries ago it was in the hands of the Ismailis, who, under Hasan Sabbah, seized the district. Now there is a legend to the effect that the Nizam-ul-Mulk, the famous Vizier, was a school-fellow of both Omar Khayyam and Hasan Sabbah; and the three youths bound themselves by an oath, sealed with blood, that whichever among them became powerful, would aid the other two.

When the Nizam-ul-Mulk rose to be Vizier, he offered Omar Khayyam the governorship of Nishapur: but the philosopher wisely declined, and, instead, asked for a pension, which was granted to him.

Hasan Sabbah, who was ambitious, asked for a post at Court, and there intrigued against his benefactor. He was, however, found out and fled to Egypt, whence he, later on, returned to Persia, where he founded his famous sect of disciples.

It is stated that the devotees of the sect were given hemp, and when under its baleful influence were carried into a terrestrial paradise with beauteous houris, gardens, running streams, and all other delights. After enjoying these pleasures for three days, they were again drugged and carried out; and thenceforward believed that, if they executed the orders of Hasan Sabbah, they would return and remain for ever in this paradise.

To give a single example of how they acted, I would refer to the case of Ibn Attash, who established a branch of the sect at Isfahan, and so successful was he that his followers increased in numbers most rapidly.

Just about this time numerous inhabitants of Isfahan began to disappear in a most mysterious manner, and Allah the All-wise used a poor beggar woman as the instrument whereby this wickedness was revealed. For she asked for alms at a certain house whence she heard groans proceeding; but when invited to enter she exclaimed, "May Allah heal your sick," and fled to rouse the quarter.

When the mob broke open the door they beheld some four or five hundred victims, many already dead; but a few, who had been recently crucified, were still alive. May the pity of Allah be on them!

This place of slaughter belonged to a blind man, who used to stand at the end of the long lane leading to his house crying, "May Allah pardon him who will lead this poor blind man to the door of his dwelling!" There the Ismailis seized and tortured the unsuspecting victim, who was done to death in return for a good deed. May the curse of Allah be on Hasan Sabbah and on his Sect!

Alhamdulillah! to-day the remnants of this sect, who still inhabit Kain and Nishapur, have left this path of darkness; and by the good fortune of His Auspicious Majesty, are simple villagers engaged in cultivating their land and praying for the long life of the Shah.

We presented ourselves before the Governor, an old man, who claimed descent from Nadir Shah. It is also said that his family has rendered such help to the Kajar dynasty that it will always keep the government of Tabas. His Excellency showed us kindness, and on hearing what had occurred he was very angry, and swore that he would burn Gholam Ali's father.[1] He immediately sent a body of his brave sowars, who finally captured the robber and brought him bound on his horse to Tabas; but just before he was imprisoned in the fort, he broke away bound as he was, and galloping his horse, took sanctuary in the shrine of Shahzada Sultan Husein. There, as you, O readers, probably do not know, he was safe so long as he remained within the sanctuary, and I have heard nothing since that day as to what happened.

In any case none of our stolen money or property was restored to us, although the Governor treated me with much kindness and gave me one hundred tomans, when we called to request permission to depart and to continue our journey.

For some stages we crossed a boundless salt desert, and in the middle of it was Yunusi. This village is famous all over the world, as it was here that the whale cast up the Prophet Yunus,[2] on him be Peace! In those days, as I have already mentioned, the salt swamp was a great sea, and, consequently, there is no doubt that this was the very spot where the Prophet reached the shore, and where a gourd grew and formed a shelter of greenery over his senseless frame. Truly Allah is great!

Two stages after leaving Yunusi we passed several encampments of Baluchis, who weave good carpets, and reached Mahavalat, noted for its melons, which, like many things in Persia, are unsurpassed. So delicate are they that they cannot be grown near a road, as the gallop of a passing horse would split them; and, alas! for the pleasure of the world, they cannot be carried even as far as Meshed, so tender are they; and yet so luscious and sweet that how can I represent it?

---

[1] "To burn a man's father" in Persia is the most usual threat. A burnt Mohamedan has no chance of Paradise.
[2] This is, of course, the Prophet Jonah.

However, Mahavalat was not a stage of good omen as, at it, there was nearly spilling of blood, which Allah forbid for men bound on a pilgrimage to the threshold of the holy Imam.

H. R. Sykes, phot.

BALUCH NOMADS

It happened in this wise. Ever since we had been robbed at Rizab, Mohamed Riza Khan, the son of Assad Ullah Khan, had every day by hints and insinuations cast reflections on the courage of the Kermanis in the presence of Ali Khan; moreover, he said that, had one of his grooms been watching instead of the two servants of Mahmud Khan, the calamity would never have befallen us. In short, there was ill-feeling between these two hot-headed youths.

On this occasion, Ali Khan said to Mohamed Riza Khan, "If you grant me permission, I will tell you how in Kerman we have knowledge of the bravery of the men of Fars. Some years ago, Isfandiar Khan, Buchakchi, the chief of one of our small tribes, entered Lar with about twenty of his fellow-tribesmen, and stated that he had the orders of His Auspicious Majesty to collect the revenue. The men of Lar at first swore that they would resist, but when Isfandiar Khan ordered his Mirza to write a telegram to the 'Foot of the Throne,' to the effect that the Laris were rebellious, they at once ate dirt and paid the revenue to the crafty brigand, so that when the Governor-General of Fars sent his servants to levy the taxes, behold Lar was as naked as the Lut, for Isfandiar Khan had clean eaten it up.

"Well, the Governor-General came with a large force to capture Isfandiar Khan, who, at first, sent polite messages to His Excellency; but, at length, he grew tired of being pursued like a fox, and said openly that there would soon be a 'Night of blood.'

"The Shirazis heard this, and that night the brave Governor-General had a deep hole dug in his tent in which to hide under the felts should an attack be made. However, nothing happened until six hours of the night had passed, when the Shirazis heard the thundering of horses' hoofs and thought that the Day of Judgment had come. Immediately they all fled, crying Aman, or quarter; but the thunder of hoofs came ever nearer, and, at last, it was seen that the lionhearted Shirazis were fleeing from a herd of mares which had been attracted by the camp fires."

As Ali Khan finished this story, Mohamed Riza Khan leaped at him like a leopard, and had not Mahmud Khan and I hastened to the spot, Allah knows what would have happened. As the Arab proverb runs, "Jesting is the forerunner of evil."

After quitting Mahavalat, we rode on hour by hour until at sunset we reached Turbat-i-Heidari, so termed after the saint known as the "Pole of Religion." Holy indeed was he who, alone of mortal men, clothed himself in felt in summer, and passed frequently through fires, and who, to still further mortify his body, slept without any covering in the "Forty days of Cold." In short, "The Chosen of Allah are not Allah, but they are not separate from Allah."

Upon our arrival at Sharifabad, which you should know is but one stage from Meshed the Holy, we found all the rooms in the caravanserai and houses already occupied by pilgrims from Tehran. Indeed, we had almost lost hope of finding any accommodation, so great was the throng, when we were met by a handsomely clad Sayyid, who accosted us in a very friendly manner with "Welcome, Khans of Kerman, you need be under no apprehension about your quarters, as they are ready."

TURBAT-I-HEIDERI

Needless to say, we were very much gratified to see that our reputation had preceded us even to this distant part of the country, and followed our guide to a small house with a garden which appeared most delightful to us after nearly two months of travel.

We quitted Sharifabad early in the morning, and even our very horses seemed to go faster, as if they felt that this was the last stage to Meshed the Holy. We crossed green, rounded hills, and at last one of our chief desires was fulfilled, for we had reached the highest ridge, known as the "Hill of Salutation"; and the golden dome of Meshed, the Glory of the Shia World, lay before us.

In the centre of the fertile valley of the Kashaf Rud we could see the Holy City surrounded by green gardens resembling emeralds, out of which rose the ineffable sheen of the unsurpassed dome with its peerless golden minarets; in truth so bright was its glory that we could not continue to gaze on it.

Meanwhile, the Sayyid spread a handkerchief and began to recite a prayer which we repeated after him, "Peace be on you, the members of the Prophet's family, the Seat of the Messenger of Allah, the Centre of the Angels, the Abode of the Angel Gabriel, the Mine of the blessings of Allah, the Guardians of Knowledge . . . . Peace be on Thee, O the greatest Stranger of all the Strangers, [1] the Sympathiser of the souls, the Sun of the Suns, buried in the soil of Tus." We then all shook hands and threw money into the handkerchief, and as I saw Assad Ullah Khan give a two kran piece, I threw down a piece of gold just to teach him that it was not the time to be parsimonious.

There were seven or eight other parties of pilgrims like ourselves on the hill. Amongst them was a merchant from Yezd, who was beaming with happiness and shaking hands and receiving congratulations. We were informed that his wife, faithful to her vow, that if her husband took her to the Sacred Shrine she would forego her dowry rights to a large landed estate, had transferred her claim to her husband. Indeed, it is a common act of piety with ladies, who after a life of longing have prevailed upon their husbands to bring them to Meshed, to forego their claim to their dowries on catching the first glimpse of the Holy Shrine.

Hundreds of returning pilgrims too tarried on the hill to say their last prayer with the golden dome in view, and to pile up stones as a remembrance. It is customary for all such parties to say "We petition for prayers," and thus to beseech pilgrims going to the Shrine to pray for them there. In reply, the hope is expressed that their pilgrimage has been accepted.

On reaching Turuk, one and a half farsakhs from Meshed, we drank a cup or two of tea and then entered carriages provided by our friend the Sayyid. Between Turuk and the Holy City we saw some huge rocks, whose weight Allah alone knows; and Sayyid Mirza Ali stopped the carriage, and pointing to their rounded shape, explained to us that these inanimate objects were like ourselves, bound from distant regions to kiss the threshold of His Highness the Imam.

As Ali Khan, who is, you must know, merely a youth, looked as if he doubted this fact, the Sayyid said to him, "O brother, thou shouldest build thy house of belief on the foundations of faith, otherwise thy house will

---

[1] In allusion to the Imam having died away from his own country.

fall." He then asked us if we had not heard of what happened to the Prophet Musa, on him be peace! who in a like case was tempted to belittle faith.

By the orders of Allah he visited a hermit, and found the holy man deep in prayer and rubbing his face on the ground. He explained to the Prophet that by such works alone could salvation be secured.

The Prophet, inspired by Allah, asked the hermit whether it were possible to pass one's finger through the eye of a needle; but the hermit rebuked him sternly for asking such a foolish question.

The Prophet then visited a second hermit whom he found in tears. Upon inquiry, the holy man said that he hoped, by humility and faith, to secure salvation, but not by works. Again the Prophet put the same question; and again he was rebuked, but this time for doubting the power of Allah, who could pass a camel or an elephant, or the whole eighteen thousand worlds, through the eye of an ant, which is much smaller than that of a needle.

The Sayyid ended his homily with the following verse:

Do not think that thou art pleasing the King by serving him; but be thankful that he has accepted thee as a servant.

To this Ali Khan made no reply, and you, O readers of London and of the New World, revere our ancient faith, and do not forget that it is only the Moslems, the Christians, and the Jews who are People of the Book.

Upon approaching the Holy City we saw mighty walls with massive towers, and crossing a handsome stone bridge we entered the "Lower Avenue" gate. The "Avenue" of Meshed is so famous for its crystal stream, its superb plane trees, and its great width, that I need not mention its perfections; but one thing I must state, which is that, even on the Day of Judgment, it would be difficult to see a much greater assembly of Mussulmans from the Seven Climates than I saw. To give a list would be impossible.

THE "LOWER AVENUE"
(With Shrine in background)

We were driven to a house in the "Upper Avenue," which was to be our residence in the city, and there partook of breakfast. After this we composed ourselves to sleep, and on waking found our mules had arrived.

With haste our servants opened our boxes and took out new suits of clothes which we had purchased in Tabas. We then proceeded to the hammam and, thoroughly refreshed, we gave our travelling clothes to the attendants, and were at last ready to cross the Sacred Threshold.

THE SACRED SHRINE OF THE IMAM RIZA

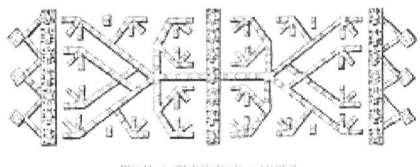

FROM A TURKOMAN CARPET

In the presence of the King what should he said but "I am ready?"
-It is not befitting to say, "Peace be on thee":
This is the most sacred spot, respect it:
It is the holy Throne of Allah, remove thy shoes.

Perhaps there is no harm, O ye wise men of Europe, if, before I act as a guide to the Sacred Threshold, which no one except a Mussulman can cross, I give you some preliminary instruction to prepare you for the glory and splendour which I shall describe to you.

Now, many of you, I dare say, are not aware that Iskandar traversed the valley of the Kashaf Rud, and that it was revealed to him that, on the site now occupied by the Shrine, one of the holiest men of all time would be buried.

To honour the spot Iskandar enclosed the land with a wall, and for many centuries the prophecy was unfulfilled, until Harun-al-Rashid, the accursed, heard of it, and, when about to die, ordered his servants to bury him and erect a dome over his body on this site. His instructions were carried out and the dome still exists, with the body of Harun-al-Rashid buried beneath it.

THE IMAM TAKING THE POISONED GRAPES FROM THE CALIPH

I now approach, with feelings of grief, the subject of our Imam Riza, on Him be Peace, who was the eighth in descent from Ali, and who was of such transcendent virtue that Mamun, son of Harun-al-Rashid, made him heir-apparent to the Caliphs, who, the Curse of Allah be on them, had hitherto slain or poisoned almost all the ancestors of the immaculate Imam.

Mamun not only coined money on which both their names appeared, but he even ordered that the sacred green of the Imam should be substituted for the black worn by the sons of Abbas. Truly, the rejoicings of the lovers of the Prophet's household knew no bounds, and they thought that "The discharged water had returned to the stream, and that right was about to be restored to the rightful heir."

However, this accursed Caliph, hearing from Baghdad that his relations were hostile to his purpose, not only changed his plans, but, with his own hands, offered poisoned grapes to the innocent Imam.

They say that, after partaking of the grapes, the ever-blessed Imam rose to depart, whereupon Mamun the Accursed, the spawn of Iblis, said, "Whither goest thou, my cousin?" To this the Saint replied, "I go to the place to which thou sendest me."

Shortly afterwards our Lord the Imam expired, and, in accordance with his own wish, was buried in the same shrine as Harun-al-Rashid.

Owing to the ignorance of mankind the tomb of the holy Imam was neglected for many generations, until it chanced that the son of the Vizier of Sultan Sanjar was residing at Tus, at that time the capital, and trying to regain his health by hunting. It happened that a gazelle, pursued by the youth, took refuge in the tomb of the Imam, and when he urged his horse in pursuit it declined to move.

After trying every means in his power to make his horse proceed, he finally understood that he was on holy ground, so he dismounted, entered the deserted tomb, and, praying to the Imam, was miraculously healed of his malady. That very night the Imam appeared to the wife of the Vizier in a dream, and when she heard of the miraculous recovery of her son she informed the Vizier and the news reached the Sultan, who at once gave orders that the Shrine should be repaired and other buildings added to it. The garden of Sanabad, which lies close by, was also brought into cultivation once again.

From this date, although Khorasan has been ravaged again and again, the Shrine has never been deserted, and when Tus was utterly destroyed, and most of its inhabitants massacred by the pitiless Moghuls, the remnant gathered round the tomb of the Imam, which has now been the capital of Khorasan for many cycles of years.

Among those who honoured themselves by giving gifts to the Shrine, was Shah Rukh, the son of Amir Timur, who presented a candelabrum of pure gold; but Gauhar Shad Aga, his wife, who, as I shall detail later on, built many of the glorious buildings, far surpassed her husband, her name being honoured to this day.

After the death of Shah Rukh confusion again ensued, and the savage Uzbegs from Khiva captured the holy city and murdered men, women, and children, not even sparing the Sayyids. They also carried off the golden candlesticks and lamps, and stripped the Shrine of its jewels and carpets, and, worse than all, they destroyed its priceless library.

After this gloomy night, however, the dazzling sun rose high in the heaven, and the Safavi dynasty, descended from the holy Imam, completed this glorious pile of buildings which form the marvel of the world. Inshallah, I will conduct you thither.

The Shrine, needless to say, forms the centre or heart of Holy Meshed, and all around it for some distance lies the property of the Imam, who is still living. In proof of this I could mention that when the Pivot of the Universe, the deceased Nasir-u-Din Shah, had constructed a telegraph line from the capital to the Sacred City he addressed the first message to the ever-living Imam, who graciously vouchsafed a reply.

To continue, you may well comprehend that all the property belonging to the Imam is sacred, and that all those who flee from injustice receive sanctuary, once they are inside the chains which hang across the road.

To make everything clear to even the ignorant, I procured a plan of the Shrine prepared by the architect, Haji Muavin-u-Sanaia. This pious individual, in order to render service to the Imam, worked incessantly to prepare this plan for a space of two years, and, hearing of this, our renowned Shah bestowed on him the high title of "Adjutor of the Architects." In short, I, after a careful examination of the plan, can state that it is correct.

Looking then at it, you must understand, O readers, that we approached the Sacred Threshold from the "Upper Avenue," and stooped to pass the chain, which we touched with our hands and then kissed, while our guide recited an appropriate prayer.

Inside on both sides were shops which are famous throughout Asia; and I am ready to confess that although the Kermanis excel all others in weaving and in many other ways, their shops cannot be compared with those of Meshed. However, this is not due to superior ability on the part of the Khorasanis, but simply to the fact that Meshed is near Bokhara, Samarcand, and also Herat; and, indeed, I found upon inquiry that the beautiful silks which I saw all came from Bokhara. The Turkoman carpets, too, which are very fine, are not produced in Khorasan. I will, however, praise its fruit, which is very good, albeit, owing to the cold, there are no figs or pomegranates grown in the gardens near Meshed.

THE "OLD COURT," SHOWING NADIR'S FOUNTAIN IN THE FOREGROUND

The Sayyid would not allow us to delay, nor indeed did we wish to, and very soon we passed through a lofty gateway, with an inscription warning the pilgrim that he was approaching holy ground, and were informed that the court of dazzling richness which we had entered was the "Old Court."

Being a lover of history I examined everything in detail, and if I tell you that the court was some ninety by sixty metres, with four great porches, and that it was covered with tiles of many colours which not only cannot be made except by Persians, but require the sapphire blue of the sky of Iran to show them in their perfection, you may faintly imagine its beauty. It is paved with hewn stones, and underneath lies the dust of thousands of pious Mussulmans.

The court is two-storied, the upper row of chambers being occupied by the high officials of the Shrine. The lesser officials, such as the carpenter, the goldsmith, and the repairers of the holy Korans, occupy the lower chambers, some of which have even been converted into tombs.

There are four porches, the most beautiful of which is known as "The Golden Porch of Nadir." It was indeed built by Sultan Husein, but was enriched by the mighty Afshar, may Allah forgive him, who not only paved and panelled it with white marble brought from distant Maragha,[1] but covered the walls with tiles cased in gold.

The inscription in great golden letters on a blue ground is very perfect, and, Allah knows, Nadir was a World Conqueror and a Lord of Perception, albeit cruel.

Of his power of perception they relate that one day when he entered the Sacred Shrine he saw a blind man invoking the aid of the Imam, and upon inquiry he learned that he had been there for several months. The Great Monarch asked him why his faith was so weak that his sight had not been restored, and swore that if on his return he found him still blind he would cut off his head. The wretched man prayed so fervently, and fixed his mind so intently on the Imam, that within a few minutes his sight was restored, and in honour of the miracle the bazaars were illuminated.

THE GOLDEN PORCH OF NADIR SHAH
(With group of Europeans)

---

[1] Maragha is near Tabriz, and over 1000 miles distant from Meshed.

Upon entering the court we first performed our ablutions at the famous "Fountain of Nadir." This unique fountain is formed from a single block of white marble decorated with exquisitely chiselled flowers; it is octagonal in shape, three feet in height, and eighteen feet in circumference. The top is hollowed out, and copper cups are suspended for drinkers; above it is a gilded cover.

They say that Nadir saw this stone at Herat, and agreed to pay a large sum for its transport to Meshed in twelve days, which, for a distance of sixty-five farsakhs, would be very difficult.

Yet, urged by the hope of a royal reward, the man brought the stone in nine days and presented himself before Nadir full of hope and happiness. The Shah, however, upbraided him for not keeping his contract and blinded him. His descendant was the owner of the house we were lodging in, and I am convinced of the truth of this story. In short, I have by these two examples shown to you both the perfect perception and also the cruel nature of Nadir Shah, the Conqueror of Delhi.

To complete my description of this court, there are two unrivalled minarets which are also cased in gold. Indeed, when the pilgrim stands where he can see the Golden Porch, the minarets, and the dome, he has no breath left in him; and it was only at my second visit that I noticed that round the dome were two inscriptions by Shah Abbas and Shah Suliman respectively. The Safavi dynasty is too famous to need praise from me. As they say, "Our enduring record is engraved in the history of the world."

After admiring the glorious blue tiling and the Golden Porch, we approached a grating of steel covered with brass, through which we could see the sacred haram.[1] This we touched, and then bowing towards the Shrine, left our shoes at the Kafshkan, which was in charge of a man who really seemed to be worthy to be a Vizier, as, although hundreds of pairs of shoes are always in his charge, he apparently never forgets to whom they belong!

Leaving, then, our shoes to the care of this individual, we entered the passage leading into the Porch of Nadir, and saw that on both sides were silver-plated doors. Traversing the corner of the Porch we entered a second

---

[1] Haram is the name for the sacred tomb chamber.

"Fountain House," in which is a large tank hewn out of a single piece of marble. Under the dome lie the remains of the favourite eunuch of Gauhar Shad Aga. They say that this individual was so honest that he was entrusted with all the money expended on these buildings by his mistress; and that when he died it was proved that he had not accumulated any wealth whatever. As the poet sings:

A black slave is often by his character whiter than others,
And a musk-coloured body has often a heart pure as camphor.
This dark colour then resembles the pupil of the eye, which is termed black,
But which is, nevertheless, its light.

From this building we entered the Dar-ul-Siada or "Place of Greatness," and surely it is worthy of its name. Its extreme length is one hundred feet, and in the middle it rises to a central dome, with a smaller dome at each end. Its decoration consists of a panelling of blue and gold tiles; and above, the wall and ceiling are covered with glass facets resembling diamonds, which, were not the chamber dark, would make the gazer blind. Set in the wall is the round golden dish from which the immaculate Imam, on him be Peace, had partaken of the poisoned fruit. In the centre of it is a hole from which ignorant people extract a little dust and rub it on their eyes, believing it to be the very dust of the holy Imam.

Here also the Sayyid drew our attention to a second grating which is made of silver, and was presented by the father of the deceased Kawam-ul-Mulk of Shiraz, whose ancestor, Haji Ibrahim, was boiled to death by Fath Ali Shah.

This Haji Ibrahim was the famous Vizier of Aga Mohamed Shah, whom he joined at Kerman after deserting Luft Ali Khan Zand. So powerful was he that the far-seeing Shah advised his successor not to trust him, but to put him to death on a suitable occasion.

At this period almost all the governorships in Persia were held by his sons, but such devoted servants had the Shah, that they were all seized on the same day at the same hour; and Haji Ibrahim was thrown into a cauldron of boiling oil as a punishment for his many crimes.

Looking through the silver grating, we, once again, saw the Imam's tomb, and once again we bowed towards it; and, burning with desire, we hastened on by the gate of the Hissam-u-Saltana, which is also plated with silver, to the Dar-ul-Huffaz, or "Place of the Reciters," [1] which resembles the "Place of Greatness," but is not so magnificent.

THE TOMB CHAMBER

Here we prostrated ourselves, touching the ground with the sides of our face, as in honour of Allah alone may the forehead touch the ground; and we prayed in accordance with the verse of the Holy Koran, "O believers, do not enter the house of the Prophet without the permission of its owner."

At last, thanks be to Allah, we moved forward and again prostrated ourselves, rubbing our faces on the threshold of the Golden Gate, one of

---

[1] The exact meaning is that the man knows the Koran by heart and has the title of Hafiz. To-day, in Persia, this title is unknown, whereas a Hafiz is highly honoured by Sunnis.

the marvels of the world. We then rose, overjoyed to be inside the haram, and, approaching the grating round the tomb, shook it, with prayers and entreaties to His Highness the Imam, and kissed it. We also kissed the lock, and you must know that every pilgrim, after handling and kissing the lock on his own account, and that of his dead relations, must do likewise on behalf of his living relations and friends, whose petition to visit the Shrine in person is thereby placed before His Highness.

I must now tell you that when the immaculate Imam died, it was desired by Mamum to bury him under the dome in the centre of the building, that his accursed father might attain his salvation from the contact of his body with that of the sacred Imam; but no tool could break open the Caliph's tomb, may the curse of Allah be on him! And, lo! a miracle befell as, while the workers were toiling in a discouraged fashion, they suddenly saw a grave ready dug in the north-east corner, and there the innocent martyr was buried with his feet towards the head of Harun-al-Rashid, the accursed.

The richness of the Shrine is unspeakable. The price alone of the door facing the foot of the tomb is worth the revenue of seven kingdoms, as it is of pure gold. The floor is inlaid with the choicest slabs of coloured marble from Shandiz, and the walls are covered with tiles in white, blue, and gold, like the work of China. Above them there is glass facet work of such beauty that how can I represent it?

The tomb of the accursed Caliph is beneath the earth and is nowhere visible, but round the tomb of the sacred Imam are three gratings. The outer of these is of steel, the one next beneath was, they say, taken from Nadir's tomb, and is of silver, studded with rubies and emeralds: the inmost grating is also of steel inlaid with gold. Above the tomb are hung jewelled aigrettes, daggers, swords, and other offerings of such value that the treasure of Karun [1] is nothing in comparison.

We pilgrims, after kissing the blessed lock, moved round to "The Foot of the Saint," and here, after prostrating ourselves close to a second gold-plated door, which is studded with rare jewels, the appropriate prayer was read.

---

[1] Karun, the Korah of the Old Testament, corresponds to the Croesus of the Greek world.

Continuing on, we moved slowly and solemnly round to "Behind the Head," facing the "Old Court." Thence by a narrow passage to "The Head."

THE GOLDEN DOOR AT THE FOOT OF THE TOMB

In the passage all the enemies of the Imam are cursed, and Sayyid Mirza Ali called out, "A curse be on Harun and on Mamun!" to which we responded, "Let it be more!" At the head of the tomb the grating was again kissed, and, after prostrations, the two prayers were read.

Thrice was the tomb encircled and thrice were the curses pronounced, after which, with tears of joy and in deep humility, we each lifted up our hands to heaven and said: "O Allah, accept my prayers and receive my praises of Thee and bind me to thy chosen people." Thus, at last, was fulfilled the great desire of my life.

THE PILGRIMAGE IS ACCEPTED

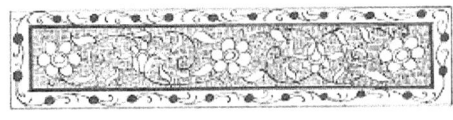

FROM A METAL LANTERN

Thanks be to Allah! whatever my heart yearned for,
Has, at last, appeared from behind the curtain of fate.

UPON returning to our lodging, I was visited by Mirza Hasan Ali, a relative of mine, who greeted me with the utmost respect and warmth. I would mention that he himself is a poet of no mean qualities, and also a learned historian; but, alas! to-day, in Iran, His Majesty is too much busied with the affairs not only of his own empire but also of every corner of the world, where his royal representatives reside, to be able to reward his poets. Indeed, when I tell you that Mirza Hasan Ali scarcely ever writes poetry, but is occupied in trying to make money out of a coal mine, where many men have already lost their fortunes, you will understand that the times have clashed together.

I was much pleased, however, to make the acquaintance of a kinsman, whom I had heard of for many years, and who I now learned had the peculiarity of never finishing the house he lived in, for fear that, once the house was completed, he would die.

But I must not forget that my readers are anxious for a description of some other of the magnificent buildings of the Sacred Threshold, and so I will ask them to accompany me to the "New Court." This splendid edifice was commenced by Fath Ali Shah of the Kajar dynasty, and was enriched by Nasir-u-Din Shah, may Allah pardon him!

MIRZA HASAN ALI, THE POET

The portico leading to the Shrine is termed the "Nasiri Golden Porch" in honour of the great Shah, Nasir-u-Din, who paved it with beautiful marble, and covered the walls with golden tiles which dazzle the eyes.

After the Shrine there is nothing in Meshed which can be compared with the mosque of Gauhar Shad Aga, who was, as has been already mentioned, the wife of Shah Rukh, son of dread Amir Timur, Lord of the Conjunction of the Planets.

In the centre of the noble quadrangle is the unroofed mosque of the "Old Woman." The story runs that when Gauhar Shad Aga, may Allah forgive her, wished to purchase the land in order to erect the mosque thereon, an old woman refused to sell one plot, but demanded that on it should be built a separate mosque bearing her name. So great was the love of justice of the Princess that her petition was agreed to, and thereby two women have obtained undying fame, the one for her piety and the other for her justice.

Now, O ye wise men of Europe, what is better than justice, and what monarchs can the world produce to compare with Faridun, of whom the poet wrote: This same monarch bequeathed the following advice to his descendants as a priceless legacy:

Faridun the noble was not an angel;
  He was not formed of musk and ambergris.
From justice and generosity he obtained his reputation.
  Do thou justice and show generosity, thou art Faridun.

Deem every day in thy life as a leaf in thy history;
Be careful, therefore, that nothing be written in it unworthy of posterity.

A nobler maxim than this no one has heard. But Faridun was not the only monarch of Iran renowned for justice throughout the Seven Climates. For it is narrated that Omar, who was subsequently second Caliph, and Muavia, who was the first monarch of the Omayyad dynasty, visited Madain, then the capital of Iran, during the reign of Noshirwan. One of the King's sons wished to purchase a mare belonging to them, but they refused to sell it at any price, and, ultimately, it was forcibly taken from them by the servants of the prince.

The strangers complained to Noshirwan, who inquired into the case, and finding their complaint to be well founded, the mare was returned to them with rich gifts from the king.

Upon leaving the city on their return journey they saw the corpse of a quartered man on the gate; and asking for what crime this sentence had been passed, were informed that the corpse was that of one of the King's sons who had taken a mare by force from some strangers.

THE MOSQUE OF GAUHAR SHAD

Many years passed, the kingdom of Persia had fallen into the hands of the Arabs, and Muavia was Governor of Syria. There he behaved in a tyrannical manner, and seized some property unjustly. Complaint was made to Omar, who was now the Caliph, and he, finding that the charge was true, wrote to Muavia a letter of one word, and that word was "mare."

The wretched man was preaching the Friday sermon in the mosque of Damascus when the epistle was delivered, and on reading it he fainted and nearly died from fear; and when he recovered consciousness he immediately restored tenfold what he had taken by force. Thus was the justice of Noshirwan a shining light to the Seven Climates, and, moreover, there is a tradition to the effect that the Prophet, on him be Peace, considered that his own birth during the reign of so just a monarch was auspicious.

To resume, there are four porches in the mosque of Gauhar Shad Aga, which are considered to be unsurpassed for elegance of construction, for loftiness, and for perfection of proportion. The tilework, too, is so beautiful that how can I represent it?

In the Aiwan-i-Maksura, above which rises the superb blue dome, stands an exquisitely carved wooden pulpit of especial sanctity, as, when the Day of Judgment is at hand, the twelfth Imam will descend on to it. May Allah hasten his advent; and may He grant that we may ever keep the Day of Judgment in remembrance!

But before quitting the Sacred Threshold I would refer to Allah Verdi Khan, who is honoured by being buried in a building adjoining the haram. This individual was a noted general of Shah Abbas, and ordered his tomb to be built during his lifetime. When it was completed the architect came to him, settled the account, and then said, "The dome is completed and only awaits Your Excellency's august body." The great noble considered this to be a message from Allah the Omnipotent, and four days after hearing it he expired.

I will now refer briefly to the famous colleges of Meshed, sixteen in number. In each of them students are provided by the legacies of pious men, not only with spiritual and intellectual knowledge, but even with food and, in some cases, with clothing.

In these colleges there are twelve hundred students, not only from every province of Persia, but also from distant India and still more distant Tibet.

Each student attends classes beginning with syntax and ending with jurisprudence, theology, and philosophy. This course, which is termed "superficial," lasts nine years, after which the student proceeds to Najaf, where for a second period of similar length he attends the lectures of the famous doctors of law.

Finally, when considered sufficiently instructed, he receives a written certificate, sealed by the principal doctors of law, to the effect that he has acquired learning equal to their own, and is a fit interpreter of the law, in which it is no longer lawful for him to follow the opinion of another. He then returns to his home, where he speedily acquires a good practice.

Among these colleges is one situated in the "Upper Avenue," which was endowed by a certain Fazil Khan, who acquired his wealth in India. One of the conditions he left in the deed of endowment was that neither Indians, Mazanderanis, nor Arabs were to be admitted. Indians because they were miserly, Mazanderanis because they were quarrelsome, and Arabs because they were dirty and unmannerly.

It is stated that an Arab applied for admittance, and upon learning the reason why he was excluded, exclaimed, "May Allah bless thy father, O Fazil Khan, for thou hast spoken the truth!"

Yet another college was endowed by a Persian, who gained his wealth in a remarkable manner. One day a rich merchant asked him whether he was willing to work at a place to which he would be conducted blindfold. Being a fearless Kermani and very poor he agreed, and was led through many streets to a courtyard where the bandage was removed, and he was ordered to dig a hole and bury gold coins and jewellery. This he did for several days, and being searched before he left, he saw no chance of bettering his condition.

However, one day he saw a cat, which he killed and ripped open. He then sewed up some money and jewels inside it and threw it over the wall. After this, when his work was done, he wandered about until he found the cat, and not only secured the money hidden in its body, but also learned the position of the house.

Its owner shortly afterwards died, and the astute Kermani bought his house with the gold sewn up inside the cat, and as the merchant had never revealed his secret to any one he became his heir, and in turn, when dying, bequeathed his money for the pious task of founding and maintaining a college. May Allah pardon him!

More than one of these colleges, these seats of the deepest learning, were visited by me, and when I saw the eager students gathered round wise, white-bearded professors, and listened to the wisdom that flowed like honey from those learned lips, I thanked Allah that he had ordained Meshed to be a "Lamp of Guidance."

After visiting all the centres of sacred interest, Mirza Hasan Ali agreed one day to guide me to the tomb of Firdausi at Tus, as it would not have been befitting for me to leave Khorasan without first honouring myself by such a visit.

Tus is situated some four farsakhs from Meshed by the Kashaf River, and, even from a long way off, its ancient walls and towers were most conspicuous. Approaching the ancient city we descended to the banks of the river, and crossed it by the famous bridge which is connected with the great poet.

As I have previously mentioned, Sultan Mahmud treated Firdausi with great miserliness; but, some years later, he was riding with his Vizier, and the question turned on whether a certain chief would submit or have to be attacked. The Vizier, by way of answer, quoted:

And should the reply with my wish not accord,
Then Afrasiab's field, and the mace, and the sword!

"Whose verse was that?" inquired the monarch, and, on learning that it was by Firdausi, he repented of his lack of generosity, and sent him a rich gift carried by the royal camels, together with an expression of his regret. But, as the camels entered the city, they met the bier on which Firdausi was being borne to his tomb!

Passing through the ruined walls we hastened on, and at last Mirza Hasan Ali pointed me out the spot where the poet lies. But, alas for the honour of us Iranis! there was no dome to mark where Firdausi, the glory of Iran, was buried, and not even a tombstone.

Allah knows how I wept for the disgrace which I, as a poet, felt most keenly, and how I repeated his poems throughout the heat of the day, and more especially the lines:

All had been dead for ages past;
But were restored to life by my poetry:
I, like Jesus, have infused life
Into all of them with my verse.
Inhabited buildings will be ruined
By rain and the revolution of the Sun:
I, however, with my poetry have reared a noble edifice
That neither wind nor rain can harm.
This poem will pass through many cycles:

And all those who possess wisdom will read it.
I have undergone many hardships during thirty years,
But have brought Persia back to life with my Persian [1] poetry.

At length, wearied out by the journey and my emotions, I fell asleep, and, in a dream, I beheld Firdausi writing his poem. Looking more closely, I saw that the poet was engaged in writing the famous story of the sons of Faridun.

It is related that when that illustrious monarch became old he gave his eldest son, Salm, the west, and Turan or Tartary to Tur; but on his youngest, Erij by name, he bestowed Iran. The two elder brothers threatened to revolt on hearing that Iran, their home and the seat of royalty, was to pass to the youngest member of the family, and Faridun was distraught at thus ending his glorious reign.

However, Erij, who was the noble son of a noble sire, heard what was the cause of his aged father's grief, and, visiting his brothers, offered to resign his crown rather than that there should be civil war. But Salm and Tur, whose mother was a daughter of Zohak, the accursed, conspired together and decided to put Erij to death.

While I gazed I saw that an angel was guiding Firdausi's pen, as he wrote the appeal of Erij to his brothers: Scarcely had the last word been written than I awoke and behold it was a dream, but I fell down prostrate on the ground and thanked Allah the Omnipotent that on me, a humble poet of modern Iran, such a signal blessing had been conferred.

Will ye ever let it be recorded
That ye, possessing life, deprive others of that blessing?
Pain not the ant that drags the grain along the ground;
It has life, and life is sweet and pleasant to all who possess it.

My last visit to the Shrine was at night, and, upon the whole, I was pleased that it was lighted with the electric light, which is, at any rate, free from objectionable matters, foreign candles being, they say, made of even the fat of the unclean animal. [2]

---

[1] The poet here boasts that he avoided the use of Arabic words.
[2] I.e. the pig.

But yet I yearned to be back in the days of Shah Abbas, who, after having performed the entire journey from Isfahan on foot, undertook the menial task of trimming the locally made candles, thousands of which illuminated the Shrine. On this occasion His Majesty was attended by Shaykh Behai, who composed the following quatrain:—

The angels from the high heavens gather like moths
O'er the candles lighted in this Paradise-like tomb:

IN THE KUHPAI DISTRICT

O trimmer, manipulate the scissors with care,

Or else thou mayest clip the wings of Gabriel.

I have not, O inhabitants of Europe, described to you the fort with its palaces, where a princely Governor-General dispenses justice and maintains such order that Khorasan is as tranquil as Kerman; nor have I described in detail the other buildings which adjoin the Shrine, for any allusion to them would, as we say, be like taking the foot of an ant into the presence of Solomon.

We had now completed our pilgrimage and had visited everything which it was right and proper to visit. We had even spent some days in the cool country of Kuhpaia, where the beautiful gardens and the running streams surpass description. In short, there was no reason for remaining any longer.

And yearning to return to Kerman took such a hold upon Ali Khan that he kept repeating:

On Friday night I started from Kerman;
I did wrong as I turned my back on my friend.

Indeed, we were all equally affected, and I quoted the verses which Rudagi sang at Herat to the home-sick Amir Nasr ibn Ahmad:

The sands of Oxus, toilsome though they be,
Beneath my feet were soft as silk to me.
Glad at the friend's return, the Oxus deep
Up to our girths in laughing waves shall leap.
Long live Bokhara! Be thou of good cheer!
Joyous towards thee hasteth our Amir!
The Moon's the Prince, Bokhara is the sky,
O sky, the Moon will light thee by-and-by!
Bokhara is the mead, the Cypress he,
Receive, at last, O mead, the Cypress tree!

No poem, perhaps, ever produced such sudden effect, as the Amir leaped on to the saddled horse, which was always kept ready for an emergency, without even donning his boots, and left his astonished courtiers to follow as best they might.

We too felt that the sands of the Lut would be softer than silk, but not in the least toilsome to pilgrims returning home from Sacred Meshed, and soon we began to make preparations for our return.

We had started on the pilgrimage in the spring time, and we left Meshed, on our return journey, at the end of the "Forty days of Heat"; and, Alhamdulillah! two months later we reached Baghin, which is but one stage from Kerman.

There we were met by many of our nearest relations and oldest friends, and Rustam Beg brought the Arab horse with the golden trappings for me to ride.

The next day, at about a, farsakh out we were met by half the city, who congratulated us so warmly and so lovingly, that, bursting into tears, I said, "Allah is my witness that Shah Namat Ullah wrote the truth when he composed the lines that "We are men of heart."

Escorted by relations and friends our joyous party entered the city and passed through the bazaars, where all the shopkeepers rose up in our honour, and so to my house. Now my house is by no means small, but when I represent that there was no room for people to stand even in the courtyard, I have explained the matter.

At last my relations and friends had wished me "May Allah protect thee," and, tired out with the long journey and my reception upon returning home, I retired to rest. But before sleep like that of the Seven Sleepers overtook me, a voice from The Unknown reached my ears, a voice of such mellifluous sweetness that its very tones brought repose to my mind. Thrice it thrilled me with the words, "Thy pilgrimage is accepted," and by the grace of the Imam, to him be praise, peace, perfect and infinite, filled my soul.

Tamam Shud,

FROM AN EARTHENWARE WATER PIPE

EPILOGUE

THE SEAL OF THE *IMAM RIZA*

The inscription on the seal runs as follows:—

Glory be to Allah
I, the Vice-regent of Allah,
Sultan Abul Hasan Ali,
Son of Musa-ar-Riza.
O Conqueror of the enemies!
O Chief of the friends
O Source of Wonders!
O Ali the Chosen!

FROM A LACQUERED PEN BOX

I was meditating how to write the date of this work
  In hidden but complete verse,
When Hatif (the Good Angel) put out his head and sang,
  "This book of travel has been speedily completed."¹

---

¹ No Persian work can be concluded without its date being shown in a verse, each letter of which possesses a numerical value. In the present instance, the number is A.H. 1331; but by a poetical conceit, the H in Hatif is "put out" or deducted, making A.H. 1326 (1908) which is the year in which the book was completed. The Persian text runs as follows:

www.ingramcontent.com/pod-product-compliance
Lightning Source LLC
Chambersburg PA
CBHW051547010526
44118CB00022B/2608